Facing Eviction and Housing Insecurity

Dayton, Ohio

Katherine Rowell, Ph.D.

The Facing Project Press

THE FACING PROJECT PRESS

An imprint of The Facing Project

Muncie, Indiana 47305

facingproject.com

First published in the United States of America by The Facing Project Press, an imprint of The Facing Project and division of The Facing Project Gives Inc., 2023.

Copyright © 2023. All Rights Reserved.

No part of this book may be reproduced, stored in a retrieval system, transmitted in any form by any means (electronic, mechanical, photocopying, recording, scanning, or otherwise) or used in any manner without written permission of the Publisher (except for the use of quotations in a book review). Requests to the Publisher for permission should be sent via email to: howdy@facingproject.com. Please include "Permission" in the subject line.

First paperback edition April 2023

Cover design by Shantanu Suman with photos by Maddie Hordinski

Library of Congress Control Number: 2023935239

ISBN: 979-8-9860961-3-1 (paperback)

ISBN: 979-8-9860961-4-8 (eBook)

Printed in the United States of America

10 9 8 7 6 5 4 3 2 1

Contents

Preface	VI
A Thank You	X
SECTION 1	1
1. Dedication and In Memorandum	5
2. Winter Vigil	7
SECTION 2	9
3. Shelter Stories	10
4. A Place to Be	11
5. My Dream: A Place to Call My Own	15
6. I Don't Know If I Can Get Through One More Winter	18
7. It's Hard to Stay Positive, But I Try to Bring Everybody a Smile	21
8. A Couple Days Turned Into a Couple Months	26
9. A Laundry List of Opportunities	28
10. It's Bigger Than a House	33
11. Burn After Reading	36

12. Not a Superhero, But	40
Section 2: Discussion Questions	43
SECTION 3	**45**
13. Stories About Eviction and Housing Insecurity	46
14. Because of This Number	48
15. Listening to Children	51
16. No Sense of Humanity	63
17. Eviction Was the Best Thing for My Family	67
18. She's Covered	70
19. 19 Times	75
20. Just Because	79
21. Desperate Times Require Desperate Measures	86
Section 3: Discussion Questions	90
SECTION 4	**92**
22. Stories From the Housing and Social Services Systems	93
23. Make Yourself at Home	95
24. Horror and Hope: Housing Insecurity Through the Eyes of a Child	99
25. We Are Fighting the System	103
26. Not Everyone Believes in Second Chances	107
27. The Bailiff Who Conducts Evictions--Be Respectful to All	111
28. From the Eyes of A Magistrate	117

Section 4: Discussion Questions	122
SECTION 5	125
29. Stories About Housing as a Human Right	126
30. Lot by Lot, House by House, Block by Block	128
31. A Righteous Fight to Eradicate Housing Insecurity	132
Final Discussion	137
Resource Guide	142
Additional Resources	144
About The Facing Project	148

Preface

"It isn't that we do not know how to budget, Miss Kathy. It is that we don't have money to budget."

Written by Kathy Rowell, Public Sociologist

Dedicated to the many women I met at the Salvation Army Shelter for Women.

Like the storytellers in this book, I have my own story and journey with this topic. In many ways, this has been a lifetime of personal and academic explorations of poverty in America. I was born into generational poverty. Like many people in Dayton, my family moved here from Kentucky for a better life. Many of my family did not choose to migrate, and many continued to live with the struggles of poverty. As a young first-generation college student, I started volunteering at a shelter for the homeless in Dayton. This decision led to numerous changes in my life, including the opportunity to work as a permanency planner for women and children in a local shelter for women, where

I helped women find housing and attempted to help them maintain it. I quickly understood that the classes on "budgeting" that I was expected to teach were not that helpful when as one woman put it, "It isn't that we don't know how to budget, Miss Kathy. It is that we don't have any money to budget with." I remember trying to find affordable housing for families, and in the late 1980s and early 1990s, there just wasn't any.

I went on to research the topic of poverty and finished graduate work at both Wright State and Ohio State in Sociology. In 1989, I published a Master's Thesis on Suburban Homeless, in which I pointed out that many suburban homeless often have to migrate to cities for help (they still do). I followed this up with research in 1994 showing that the welfare system had worked and helped many people out of poverty. Unfortunately, my dissertation was published at the same time when the Clinton Administration created " Welfare to Work Systems." No one really wanted to read a dissertation that demonstrated the system of some "cash assistance" was helping.

Over the years, I have taught about poverty, worked with numerous students at various shelters in Dayton, studied poverty, volunteered for various organizations, and written papers and articles about this issue. Teaching about poverty and increasing awareness was one way I thought I could effect change. I am thankful to have so many former students working for various marginalized communities in Dayton. We have so many good people in our community working for change.

Still, the housing systems in the United States were designed in many ways to perpetuate and maintain inequality (the recent Redlining work in our community bears witness to this). The inequitable housing systems continue to act as a form of structural violence lead-ing to issues like environmental racism, high infant mortality rates, poor health outcomes, and mental health challenges to name just a few. The lack of adequate, affordable housing leads to lower life expectancy rates for many groups in the United States. Housing is one of the most critical basic needs of everyone on this planet. It is also one of the most structurally complex systems to challenge in the United States. But, it needs to be challenged.

Many of the same issues our community faced when I was a naive undergraduate student remain. We still see a lack of affordable housing and women and children experiencing high rates of poverty and eviction. Over the years, I have witnessed many students at my college struggle with poverty. I have witnessed the growing number of people walking our streets asking for help. I witnessed the numbers in our shelters increase. I have heard politicians pontificate about plans for change. I shed tears at the annual vigil for the unhoused who died in our community.

My story is integrated with so many other stories in our community, and thus, this is the power of the story. I am thankful for those who shared their stories with me over the years. During the pandemic, we witnessed further increases in poverty and inequality in our country. I was thankful to be a member of the City of Dayton Eviction Task Force. This task force has been diligently working since 2018 to change the system. Many of us felt the need to do more. I decided to apply for a fellowship to bring some public dollars to our community to increase awareness. I am thankful for a Mellon/American Society of Learned Communities Fellowship that covered the cost of working with the Facing Project and producing this book.

The students I teach and the young people in our community continue to give me hope that change is possible. I hope these stories increase awareness and empathy and ultimately lead to discussions and actions about social change. I do not think anyone, especially children, should experience homelessness. We can and should make housing a human right.

A Thank You

This project would not have been possible without the voices of many people in our community. First, I would like to thank the many storytellers who made time in their busy lives to share their stories for this project. It is through storytelling that the invisible is often made visible. I hope this project honors your stories and, more importantly, serves as a conduit for dialogue, social change, and justice in our community. I would also like to thank all the writers for their dedication to increasing awareness about housing justice in our community.

This project was made financially possible by a Mellon/American Council of Learned Societies Community College Fellowship I received in 2022. I am thankful for the financial support that enabled us to fund this project through The Facing Project. A special thank you to the Co-Founder and President of The Facing Project, J.R. Jamison, and his staff for their insight and guidance.

I would like to thank members of the community steering committee who met numerous times from October 2022 to April 2023 to guide this project. They also served as recruiters for both stories and writers. Many of them work daily in the community doing housing justice work.

Members of the Steering Committee included:

Kate Geiselman, Chair of the English Department, Sinclair Community College

Debra Lavey, Senior Attorney, Advocates for Basic Legal Equality, Inc.

JoAnne Richardson, Outreach Specialist, Dayton Public Schools

Jenny Lesniak, Program Coordinator Housing and Homeless Solutions, Montgomery County

Jessica Jenkins, Director, Human Services and Planning Department, Montgomery County

John Zimmerman, Vice-President, Miami Valley Fair Housing

Torey Hollingsworth, City of Dayton, Director of the Office of Commission

Commissioner Carolyn Rice, Montgomery County

Jayne Klose, Dayton Metro Library

Aaron Primm, Landlord/Tenant Program Coordinator, Dayton Mediation Center

Laurel Kerr, Dayton Mediation Center

Miranda Wilson, Miami Valley Fair Housing

Melanie Cooper, Sinclair student

Emily Peck, Sinclair Student, and Research Assistant

Jaela Robinson, Sinclair Student, and Research Assistant

Erin Thomas, Sinclair Student, and Research Assistant

Additionally, I would like to thank the following organizations and people for their support of this Facing Project:

The staff of the various shelters and organizations in our community provided guidance and support for this project, and many of them served as writers or storytellers in this book.

Kate Geiselman, Chair of English at Sinclair Community College, supported and helped to edit two Facing Projects in our community.

Gina Neuerer, Chair of the Theater Department at Sinclair Community College, Daniel Brunk, Assistant Professor, and the staff and students of the department assisted with the production of the stories for the book premiere in April 2023.

Sara Kiewitz, Professor of English at Sinclair Community College, helped support my thoughts on this project.

Violet Johnston-Hobbs, Marie Jenkins, and Debra Swanson provided support and kindness as I talked through this project numerous times. I appreciate your "cheer" through this project.

Maddie Hordinski, Cincinnati, Ohio, graciously made time to come to Dayton and photograph the images for this project. You can read more about her work: https://www.madeleinehordinski.com/. A special thanks to Erik Nelson for recommending her for this project and for his support in listening to me talk through this project numerous times.

Kevin Kelly, Executive Director of the Dayton International Peace Museum, and the staff of the museum provided space and support for the writers training in November 2022.

Many friends and colleagues at Sinclair Community College, especially my mom, Joan Scott, and my adopted brother, Robert Wells, for your support and for all you do for the unhoused and hungry in the Dayton Community.

My two sons, John and Jack, spent much of their childhood volunteering with me in the community. I appreciate the empathetic individuals you have become. Thanks for understanding.

SECTION 1

In 2018, Dayton, Ohio, was listed as the 26th worst city in the United States for eviction filings (evicitonlab.org). At that time, Mayor Nan Whaley of Dayton formed an Eviction Task Force. This task force included numerous representatives from the community, including lawyers, community advocates, landlords, judges, county and city officials, and academics. Occasionally, we would have someone with lived experiences share a story, or a task force member would share a story. We learned that many community issues were increasing our eviction rate compared to other cities, including topics like "source of income" and the civil "right to counsel." Just when the work was beginning to happen, our nation was hit with a pandemic. Thankfully, the eviction task force was able to switch gears, and they continued to meet virtually and talk about issues like "rent caps," rent assistance, and the Centers for Disease Control Moratorium.

We now know that rent assistance during the pandemic significantly reduced evictions in our community. We also know that despite the moratorium on rent, racial disparity in eviction filings remained. Research by Dr. Tim Thomas indicated that the ratio for Black renters rose from 1.29 before the pandemic to 1.3 during the pandemic (https://evictionresearch.net/ohio/dayton.html). The eviction task force is an active community group that is diligently working on ways to reduce eviction in our community. Cleveland and Toledo are the only cities in Ohio to have the Civil Right to Counsel. The Civil Right to Counsel has made a difference nationwide in reducing eviction. Eviction reduction is only one challenge in the housing justice system. As noted in this collection of stories, people are experiencing many situations and life circumstances. Most issues are related to poverty and lack of affordable housing. Still, unfortunately, other issues like domestic violence, lack of adequate support for those suffering from mental health issues, and discrimination are part of this problem. Our shelters for the unhoused and those experiencing domestic violence are full, and the waiting lists for affordable housing are long. The support network is underpaid and overworked, yet they continue to strive for change.

This book is a collection of stories from various community members who wanted to share their lived experiences. The book begins with a story about a vigil for those who died unhoused in Dayton in 2022. This book is dedicated to their memory and the memory of those who have died without a place to call home. The next section of this book is a collection of voices from those who were staying in various shelters in our community. These people made time to volunteer their stories, and every single storyteller noted that they hoped this would help people understand what is happening in our community. I bore witness to each of these storytellers and their writers. I am very appreciative of their willingness to share during a time of crisis. The second set of stories comes from people who experienced various forms of housing insecurity but most of whom are thankfully housed today. I am thankful for their willingness to reflect on difficult times and to offer their thoughts on housing injustice. Quite a few books on lived experiences of the "homeless" have been shared, but I think the section with lived experiences from those working in these systems is unique. I so appreciated that people from the legal system, safety net systems, and a landlord chose to share their stories and perspectives. The housing system is complex, and they added perspectives that are helpful for social change. Finally, this book concludes with powerful stories of two women from our community fighting for housing justice. I continue to be inspired by their dedication and diligence in Dayton.

This book was meant for community dialogue and group discussions. There are guided discussion questions at the end of each section and a dialogue guide at the end of the book. There are resources provided throughout the book to learn more. There is also a resource guide provided for those seeking assistance in our community.

In conclusion, this book is a beginning. There are stories that were missed and voices that remain to be heard. More stories about housing justice, not housing injustice, have yet to be written. I look forward to reading those stories someday.

A brief note about the stories:
The writers in this story volunteered their time to listen to those with lived experiences share their stories. These stories are written in first-person by the writer to help not only share the story but to create connections of empathy. Both the writer and storyteller approved the final story. These stories are the lived experiences of the storyteller and thus are not

fact-checked but rather presented as told to the writer. Stories are often presented as directly told to the writer, and at other times writers used creative license (with permission of the storyteller) to create poetry or more creative stories. Given discrimination in the housing system, most storytellers chose to remain anonymous or use a pseudonym to protect their real identities. We appreciate those storytellers who, given their work, wanted the community to know their identity. Finally, this project is not intending to blame the "social safety net," but rather to question the housing systems that have led to the need for a social safety net. This project is meant to help us explore how we can increase affordable and adequate housing opportunities for all.

Dedication and In Memorandum

This book is dedicated to the memory of those who died unhoused or living in shelters in the Dayton Community in 2022.

Your voices and stories will not be forgotten
Alizhan I.,26....Pam A., 60....Gurney F, 58....
Steven H., 59....Deangelo W.,22....Jeanetta F.,57....
Dennis S.,61....Daryl G., 63....Pamela R., 72....
Scott M.,60....Billy A., 27....Brad S.,38....
Tyler W.,45....Tyler S., 29....Daniel B., 58....
Chad L., 51....Jewell G., 61....Jennifer A., 37....
Victor J., 61....Natasha D.,40....Jamell B., 37....
Dennis B.,49....Matthew W.,27....Kyle O., 38....

*Danny M., 56....Sherri G., 51....Robert L., 62....
Trienna W., 39....Darrell F., 58....Michael B., 54....
Anthony T., 58....Troy M.,61....Michael B., 32....
Ruby W., 61....Clyde C., 44....Anthony R., 60....
Elrond S., 39....Tammy L., 52....Steven C., 61....
Christopher J.,53....Amanda S., 36....Guy Y., 63....
Lakesha H., 28....Darryl D., 62....Marty P., 29....
Richard D., 64....Robert S., 36....Colleen M., 60....
Emmanuel G., 31....Jimmie P., 82....Bobby Y., 40....
Shawn S., 48....Roberto M., 41....Jena W., 36....
Kenyon M., 33....Mark S., 65....April B., 48....
Mario T., 37.... Keith E., 30....Benjamin L., 56.....
Lewis P., 56....Terrence M., 61....Derek Y., 63....
Michael S., 57....Lucille B., 53....Deandria W., 33....
Willie B., 56....Ted H., 56....Joshau Ann S., 46....
Athena M., 40....Gwendolyn F., 56....Judy C.,73....
Heather F., 35....Diana H., 65....Michael W., 53....
James C., 43....Sherry R., 47....Darren W., 57....
Lester B., 65....Earl F., 65....Melvin S., 63....
and Dennis M., 53....*

And for the countless others who left this earth without a place to call home.

Winter Vigil

by Kate Geiselman

It's cold on Courthouse Square, even for December in Dayton, even for the shortest day of the year. Most folks in the crowd of forty or so are bundled up in boots, hats, and warm coats, but still, they shiver in the 19-degree air. Some blow into their hands or stomp their feet to keep warm. What would it be like not to have a warm place to go after this? Or ever?

After the County Commissioner welcomes us to the vigil, the Mayor steps up to the mic. He is coatless and hatless as he speaks to the assembled crowd. If he's freezing, he doesn't show it. Eighty-seven pairs of shoes march along the top of the wall behind him, one for each person who died in 2022 due to homelessness. Each pair of shoes has a nametag attached. Jewel, Victor, Natasha. Someone's sister. Someone's son. Someone's mother.

A member of the Youth Action Board reads the poem "Four Candles." They represent grief, courage, memory, and love. The last line, "We remember you," lingers. This is why we have gathered on this frigid day: to put names to the numbers. To remember that these lives had meaning and purpose, and that these people were loved.

A representative from the VA Medical Center is next. In a voice steady and clear, she sings "I pray for a world where pain and sorrow will be ended. And every heart that's broken will be mended." Many in the crowd bow their heads. The final notes and words are suspended in the cold air: "Give us grace so we'll be safe." It's hard not to wonder whether a prayer like that was uttered by those we are here to remember, and why it wasn't answered.

It's time, now, for the litany of those who have died. Volunteers from various local agencies take turns reading their names, last initials, and ages. A bell tolls for each of them, some as young as 29, all gone too soon. One reader becomes overwhelmed with emotion. The mayor quietly comes over and puts his arm around her shoulder. She pauses to collect herself. He stays with her until she has finished reading her list, until the last toll of the bell dissipates.

A director from St. Vincent de Paul prays that the Lord will "use our tears to wash away the inequities in our society" before we join together to sing "Let There be Peace on Earth." By now, our faces are numb, but our emotions are raw. We disperse slowly; many of us pause to read the nametags on the row of shoes: crocs, sneakers, sandals, and boots. We imagine the 87 people who might have worn them. We know they are meant to be symbols, but they are tangible, both solid and empty, filled only with the cold December air.

Tomorrow, the days will start to get longer, but winter has just begun.

SECTION 2

"**D**on't try to drive the homeless into places we find suitable. Help them survive in places they find suitable."

— Daniel Quinn

These stories were told by members of our community who were staying in our shelter systems during the month of December 2022. We are thankful for their time and willingness to share. They all hoped that sharing their stories would create empathy and understanding of those struggling with housing insecurity in our communities.

Shelter Stories

A Place to Be

An anonymous story as told to A.B. Hiatt

It was up to me to rescue him
Shredded paper, twisted metal from a pencil rim,
The socket sure is sparking well--Presto!
White smoke, blackening plastic, a chemical smell.
The building burning bright, first orange, then red,
The police station fades to ash.
What went through my eight-year-old head?
Without him how long would I last?
A kid in court on account of his uncle,
Facing his own counts--one boy minus one uncle,
Less one mother, three times the struggle.
My uncle off to prison, my mother God knows where;
A child thrown to the State's tender care.
I'm shoved in a "safe" place they'd picked
While mother dearest fumbles for a grip.
Better here, they say, than in a house with her,

Where mom's nine personalities battle cancer.
***

Orphanage is another term for a lock-up;
There's bars on the windows and beds in a row;
My jailers act heaven sent;
they're just hollow arms for government.
They keep telling me it's nice here, but no one's free to go.
It's a foreshadowing of forty years' fate.
I'm bound to a path chosen by the State,
Free to suffer the consequences
Of the determinations they make.
No time to learn to strive for myself
When I'm caught in fights on my right and left.
A pack of boys, no matter how neatly dressed,
Are ruthless as a hornet's nest.
A boy must master the art of violence
When raised in a land of spite.
Gotta know how to throw hands,
When everyone is anything but alright.
At night, I try to sleep under the bed,
Eyes smashed shut, ears stretched wide
For the tell-tale echoes--
The footfalls from which I hide.
His violation leaves me unstable, out of sorts.
Suddenly I'm tossed from the orphanage,
Back to mom; more hearings in the courts; Only to land
With my militaristic ex-step-dad,
Silence after pistol-whippings the only peace I have.

Drill Sargent says I'm out of order.
By 13, it's four houses I've been kicked outta.
Wander to one house, then another,
Wonder if I'll get a call from my mother.
Maybe this time—the cancer—It finally got her?

***

The rest of my teens are spent locked up
In another facility with flashy slogans
But words are smoke as soon as they're said,
I'm locked in a closet instead of under a bed.
They say nine hours ain't the end of the world,
And the dude, himself? He won't work here no more.
But none of that makes anything alright,
I'm stuck in another lock-up filled with spite.
By rough experience or genetic design,
I split in half, my good dude and my bad guy.
I say my two ain't as bad as her nine.
I hear that's how it is till I die.

***

At last, I'm free to go.
How does one make it
Just eighteen years old?
What do I even know?

***

I find a steady income in construction.
I'm the guy who likes to sling that mud,
Bosses, they call me a natural--
For once something I'm proud of.

But it is always a matter of time,
Before I'm at wit's edge
And stretching my last dime.
Two kids and a girl ain't cheap,
Not the mouths to feed, not the roof to keep.
2007: a way to say recession.
How was anybody supposed to make it work then?
If the college boys couldn't get any
Where the fuck did the rest of us fit in?

***

There's one house where I can return after each eviction
You know, the one that's big and embarrassing to mention.
But after long roads and short funds, I'm there another time,
A trip that breaks my body the way others did my mind.
Now I'm here in the shelter, at least for tonight,
Tomorrow's roof is tonight's worry.
Will I find any food? A warm spot I can keep?
Can I trust people around here enough to sleep?
Always been 'round lots of people,
Always been alone.
All I want is a place to be,
A place to call my home.

My Dream: A Place to Call My Own

An anonymous story as told to Sean Frost

Here at the shelter, it's about your mind-frame. Are you going to show respect to earn respect? Are you going to stop stealing and learn to clean up after yourself? There're so many cats in here that just don't seem to care. They ain't going nowhere. But I've got a plan.

Yet, here I am, again. This is my fifth time living in a shelter. This place is noisy and smells bad. There's always the bustle of plates and trays, the sounds of men arguing and fighting, the TV playing some show I didn't pick. Mostly it smells like unwashed feet and dirty clothes. The stench is everywhere, and I really want my own space. Some place to call my own. Just to be able to take a nap whenever I want. Or to be able to go out and come back without worrying about my food being gone. The little things that many people take for granted every day – a clean bed, a hot shower, good food – these are the things that motivate me to get out of here!

I've been here at the shelter for three months and two weeks, this time. I am very thankful and grateful for this shelter; I can't imagine having to sleep outside. I've seen people sleeping under bridges and on benches, right here in Dayton! I can't handle that.

I'm a 46-year-old Daytonian, and my first experience with homelessness was back in 2009. After doing five years in prison, I'd been living with my dad, before he got sick and passed away. I stayed with my baby mamas at times, but that always could be tough. Sometimes I'd have to leave; I'd choose to come to the shelter rather than stay there. My mom lives in a nursing home and my older brother's not doing too well. I'd really like to be able to get out on my own and spend some time with him. One of my brothers is in here with me. We look out for each other when we can, but I've really got to worry about me. That's one of the lessons I learnt through the years is that we're in this alone. You come into the world by yourself, and you going to go out the same way.

Life at the shelter is difficult but I'm grateful. We are woken up at 5:00 every morning, breakfast at 6:30, and we must be back in before they close up for the evening. There are some guys in here that never leave. Our rooms are off-limits during the day, so guys just sit and sleep in the gym all day and only get up to get their three meals. I can't figure out these cats; some of them come from the youth shelter and then still don't want to work once they're here. They seem okay with just being here. Me? I've got a plan! There are so many people here (I crave peace and quiet) and I have made a friend or two, but I've come to realize that I'm in this alone. I spend a lot of time alone but being alone is kinda slick. No hassles, nobody wanting nothing from you.

I just want to get my own space, mind my own business. I'm sick and tired of being sick and tired. I'm always tired. I get back from work late and then we are up at 5:00. I know I've got to put in the work. I just started at my job so I'm trying to stack up my money. My case worker has helped me to apply for apartments, and I'm on waiting lists at eight different places. As soon as one of those comes through and my money's stacked up for DPL and whatever, I'll be out of here. I can have my own space, with my own food, my own odor, and my own tv, and I can have my kids and grands over and just be.

Till then I just got to keep my focus on. Don't stay down. Get up. Put in the work. Mind my own business and I'll be just fine. I've got my mind-frame in the right place.

I Don't Know If I Can Get Through One More Winter

An anonymous story as told to Stan Hirtle

I was in the hospital. The hospital lost my wallet. It had all my ID, my Social Security card, and the bank debit card where my Social Security was going.

Since then, I couldn't get my money. Social Security said see the bank. The bank says they closed my account for lack of use and sent the money back to Social Security. It has changed its name. The bank and Social Security run me from one to another and say the other is responsible. I am supposed to talk to Social Security tomorrow. I hope something comes of it.

I have had my health damaged several times. I am disabled. I was hit by a drunk driver while standing on the sidewalk. They thought I was out in the street, but I had a witness. I have iron in my legs and titanium knees. It is hard for me to walk. I went from crutches to a walker to the cane I have now. While homeless, I was beaten with a baseball bat and robbed. Last winter, I got frostbite while I was homeless on the streets. They had to amputate my toes. When I apply for jobs now, no one will hire me. They say I am a liability. They won't want to be responsible if I fall on the job. I understand that.

After I lost my toes to frostbite, I was in the hospital, then was sent to a nursing home for three months for therapy. Eventually, the medical wouldn't pay, and I was discharged to this homeless shelter. I have lived in Springfield and Columbus but do not know Dayton at all. I have been here for three weeks and expect to be here a long time.

I wasn't always on the streets. I have worked since I was 14. I served six years in the Army. I drove semis for 10 years. I drove elderly people and people in wheelchairs to their homes. I drove cabs. I worked in a pizza drive-through. I drove railroad crews to worksites. I loaded and drove supplies for a gas station franchise.

My last job was in a gas station. I slept in the rest room at night. They closed the gas station and tore it down. That was my last home. Before that, a guy let me stay in a building where he stored stuff. It had no heat, water, or electricity.

Since then, I have been on the streets. Some of us were sleeping a lot in Springfield. Some church people gave us tents. We did clean up so the police would be ok with us, but the nearby fast-food place didn't want us there and got our tents torn down.

Mostly, I hung out. Sometimes I looked for fallen change at fast food drive-throughs, so I could get a cigarette. I don't believe in begging and won't ask people for money. The panhandlers I see are young and healthy. They should get jobs.

I have no contact with my children. I have 3 daughters. She had 2 jobs to try and get by. I have no way to contact her. My first wife left me for my little brother. Another woman I was with lost her children to Children's Services. Our daughter was adopted, and I have no idea where she is.

My memory is very bad. I can't remember a lot of things. I am hard of hearing. I am stressed out. I don't know how much more I can take or whether I can get through one more winter. I have no way to get from here to downtown Dayton to go to Social Security or the church that does ID ministry. The only contact I have is a church ministry that drives me to church services.

I have an appointment with a caseworker for this shelter in two days. I hope the caseworker can help me. Otherwise, I don't know what I am going to do.

It's Hard to Stay Positive, But I Try to Bring Everybody a Smile

An anonymous story as told to Debra Oswald

I'm 25. That means I'm the youngest one here. And we're all women because it's a women's shelter.

It's hard to stay positive, but I try to bring everybody a smile. And it's kind of hard to do because it's Thanksgiving, and everybody's missing their families and loved ones. It sucks because my mom lives in West Virginia and I couldn't go visit her to spend Thanksgiving together. But she knows I'm trying to better my life.

I go by Asher. This is my second time around being here, and it will be three weeks on Friday. I am a recovering addict. I live with mental health issues. I am a sexual abuse, physical abuse, everything-you-can-think-of abuse survivor. But I am eight months clean being sober off meth. This is like my fifth time trying to stay sober because of where I was living in West Virginia. It's hard to stay sober around there because anywhere I go to I can find my stuff. So I told my mom, "Look, I have to go somewhere else, out of West Virginia, and start anew."

She said, "No matter where you go, your problems are gonna follow you."

"Yeah, that may be the case, but I have to go somewhere where I don't know anyone so I can't find meth."

I came to Dayton three months ago because I have friends here and they're helping me the best they can. At first it was just me and my brother. Well actually, he's my best friend, but we act like siblings so I might as well call him my brother. We were trying to get hotels. But we weren't keeping up with the payment. Then we started living in a rental car. We were making those payments, but then his friend was supposed to pay Enterprise for us and didn't. So, the car was reported stolen. My brother got arrested. I ended up in the shelter, and here we are.

I've been homeless off and on since I was eighteen. The first time I was homeless it was because I was going through a sexual abuse case. And I couldn't live with my mom because me and her were having problems. I was going through the sexual abuse case and I wanted to drop it because I couldn't deal with the stress. She knew I wanted to drop the case and she told me not to. We couldn't agree, so I left, and we didn't talk to each other for a few months.

I lost two of my favorite jobs because I was homeless and I couldn't find transportation. That sucked because my first job was at Dairy Queen, and I loved making kids smile. I was always making Blizzards and when kids ordered a Blizzard, I would say, "Want to see a magic trick?" and they'd say "Yeah!" and I flipped the Blizzard upside down like you're supposed to. Usually I had five to six Blizzards going out and I flipped every single one because it made me happy to see the kids smile. My second job was at a retail distribution center. But I couldn't get to my shifts because the buses don't run past 6 p.m. I tried to find another job, but being homeless and trying to get an apartment, it was basically impossible.

It's a struggle here. This shelter's filled to the max and it doesn't have pillows, blankets, good food. Like, we need decent meals and actual decent servings. It doesn't help that everyone is sick and they can't give us cold medicine and there's no cough drops. And we don't have bus passes so we can't get to the library. It's just really difficult. If I ran this place, it would be totally different. I would have free WiFi, pillows, and blankets for everybody. I would have laundry facilities upstairs and down. People just wanna wash their clothes. There's a laundry system. We put our laundry in big bags the shelter collects, and we don't see our clothes for a couple of days. One of my friends just lost a bunch of clothes with that system. We have a clothes closet where you can get free clothes, but there's a lot of plus-size people, so there's not enough plus-size clothes. That makes it even more difficult. Especially with me being transgender, I wear men's clothing. There's not enough men's clothing back there for anything. Pants, shirts, underwear, it doesn't matter. There's not enough.

I've always known that I was not a female. I never did anything girly growing up. When I was a freshman in high school, the coach asked me if I wanted to join the football team even though I had no experience. I was like, "Hell yeah! But I know somebody who won't let me. My mother. We can't afford it." He tried talking to her. He called her and said, "I will personally pick her up and take her to the games." She still said no, even though the school was going to pay for everything. The track coach also asked me to be on his team. Even though I could have walked to the field, my mom still said no. I would have been good at sports. Things could have been different. I could be sitting in college right now.

I'm going to be starting my testosterone next month. It's better to be in a women's shelter during this process. Women are more understanding about transgenders than men. You've got some men who don't understand and just think it's wrong and will fight you on it. I didn't want to put myself in that situation.

What keeps me going through all this is my son, my faith, and my friends. I'm a Norse Pagan. Thor, Loki, Odin; those are my gods. People frown upon my religion, but my friends understand. My son is four and lives in Texas. He's got two dads. I told my mom, "If I put my son up for adoption, I want a gay or lesbian couple to have him." And that's what I got. They are great parents. I couldn't ask for better.

As I said, I've been through it all. I've lived on the streets, in a car, and in shelters. I don't recommend the homeless life. It's mentally straining, it's physically straining, and you'll end up with mental health issues if you don't already have them. It's not fun. And if you're camping out in a tent, find a homeless shelter, because winter's coming.

A Couple Days Turned Into a Couple Months

An anonymous story as told to Adrienne Cassel

Where was I living? Let's just say, it was too much work. There was mold. There was heating problems. So, you know what? Instead of me just telling them, I decided to try and fix some things myself, but it just didn't work out. And so I said, this is what I am going to do, so I packed everything up, right?

I was just going to be in the shelter for a couple days. Then a couple days turned into a couple weeks. A couple weeks turned into a couple months. You know, I have been here since September/October.....I have been in here three months. I have been having some really long months here. I have my good days, then I have my bad days. What you would call stage 5 renal failure. I am a stage 5 failed renal patient. I have to go to dialysis three times a week. That's a challenge. Usually they come and get me. Yesterday, I waited, and they did not. Like I said, sometimes things go wrong. Recently, my purse was stolen from the shelter. I had my identification stolen. I felt vulnerable. It was stolen from me.

With everything else, that kind of thing...in MY position? I asked, why me? Why would you want to do this to me? I can't wait to hurry up and leave here because I can't trust anyone. It feels like I can't, anyway. I was supposed to have a meeting with one of my caseworkers today, but I fell and couldn't go. Like I said, I have been having some really long months here.

A Laundry List of Opportunities

An anonymous story as told to Emily Peck

Everyone says I have a way of telling stories. Sometimes it's a trainwreck, and sometimes it's a linear thought. I start work tomorrow at McDonald's. I owe my friend $200 for my car that's in the shop. I feel like I'm the broke best friend. She says it's okay and to just "get on my feet." She's a good friend, we've known each other since we were eleven. But she had to kick me out because her kid has a heart condition, and I was working at Rural King at the time fixing machines and working up to a manager with bonuses and everything. But with the pandemic, my friend had to protect her kid. I understand.

I've had my laundry list of opportunities and jobs. I've worked at Walmart and Subway, and CVS and was making decent money. But also, we're only human; and sometimes we just make so many bad decisions that it becomes overwhelming, and you can't even tread through the water.

I spent two and a half years in prison because of drugs. My mom gave me diet pills when I was eleven, and it quickly progressed to using crack cocaine. My mom would do drugs with me–she encouraged me. I was spiraling, but then I got pregnant with my son, and I got sober enough to have him. He spent most of his time with his aunt. I moved to Toledo and went to college. I wanted to be an art therapist and knew that going to school would help me provide for my son. I was doing well. I had an apartment through section 8 and owned my own car. Then we moved back to Dayton, and I was in Women's Recovery.

Everyone in recovery warned me not to go back down to Dayton, where my mom was. But I got an apartment and had a job at a restaurant. And then we had an eviction. I felt like I was losing everything. Like everything was spiraling, again. My section 8 housing was denied, and I knew I was going to lose my apartment. I felt helpless.

I cashed my last check in the mailbox from my job and went on a bender, and prayed, "God, if I get away with what I'm contemplating doing, separate me from the drugs." That night I robbed a store. But I didn't even spend any of the money. I was found face down in front of my apartment with a gun to the back of my head by a cop, and I said to God, "If I can survive it, I can do better."

And I did.

I went to the Greene County jail, and I got sober. I went to every program that the jail offered to fill my time. Bible study, classes, you name it. I was there. I focused on my promise to God to get my life right in that Greene County jail.

When I got out, I went to a halfway house because I had such good behavior. Then I married my husband. Not soon after, he broke his leg at work and had to take time off. With no income coming in, we lost our studio apartment and had to go to two separate shelters.

And so it's almost like you have to be destitute and in a situation where you can't focus on anything else but housing... it's overwhelming.

Eventually, we got it back together and had an apartment. For a year, I was sober. And for a year, he was lying to me. One night I got off work, got home, and watched him have a seizure. Up and down, up and down. Like a rollercoaster. I thought he was joking for a second. But he had a massive heart attack and died.

Turns out he had been strung out on pills. For a year, he had been lying when I was struggling to stay sober.

I used to have dreams. I wanted to be an art therapist. And then a welder, and then a teacher. My mother was a teacher. And so was my grandma.

Now my life felt like it was falling apart.

In May, my son got stabbed. He was fighting with kids he shouldn't have been hanging out with, and the mom of one of the kids stabbed him in a Taco Bell parking lot. I was calling everyone I knew, trying to get them to drive me to the hospital to see him, but no one wanted to help me because of my past, asking for help and using it to buy or get drugs. But I just needed to make sure my son was okay.

When I got to the hospital, my son wanted to see me. Usually, my son chose his aunt, but he kicked all of them out. He wanted me that night, and I got to wash his hands to get the pepper spray out and nurture him. I hated seeing him in so much pain, but at the same time, I got to take care of him, like a mom.

I wanted to hurt the lady who hurt my son. But on the way back, I just kept thinking, *I'm the killer I'm the killer I'm the killer*, and I was going back into that old thing and old patterns that I'd fallen into and not really valuing my life and God said, "You need to be there for your kid and your grandbabies. You need to be on this side of the fence for your son. You need to make better choices so that you can be there. Because you have chosen things over him. Choose him this time." And so I think a lot about that. Our healing and our being able to talk to each other is because of that night.

You know? My mom did drugs with me, and there are a lot of things I did wrong as a mom, but I swore I would never do a crime with my son. He was in with some bad "friends," and I had to tell him, "You can't pull one on me; you're smarter and better than that."

I've worked hard to stay on the right side of the fence, and it's so much harder once you've messed your life up; to get your life right because people are always judging you and thinking that you're out to get them and it takes a lot of breaking of bad habits. I want better for my son, so I must be better.

Times are hard. It's not just drug addicts that end up in this situation; there are people who have real drug issues that end up on this side of the shelter.

You know, when I was in high school, I raised money for Daybreak and this shelter. I got washrags and care packages dropped off here from Cub Foods and Kroger's. But now, I didn't have nothing to get my son when he turned 18 this year, but I used to write letters to him when he was really little and put them in the photo albums, and on his 18th birthday, I read some of them to him. But what's beautiful is his response to that was, "Love you, mom, that means a lot to me."

That made me cry when he said that.

It's Bigger Than a House

Marilyn's story as told to Keisha Anderson

You could give me a house right now and that wouldn't solve my problems. Umm first, I need- I need counseling. Fo'sho. And Umm I mean I jus wanna be able to jus let everything go. I want the people in the world to know to never give up, umm always be strong. Don't let nobody belidal, how you say, belittle you? And jus umm happy. To get back the joy that I've loss. That's what I want.

So I ended up being homeless due to a domestic violence situation uh about a month ago. Umm I waited until he left home and I just ran with me and kids, and I called around with a neighbor and she leaded me here to this shelter. So... Umm Sometimes I wonder if my kids love me the same or blame me for us being homeless. I need them to know that I will always love them and that I will always fight for them. No matter what the situation may be. And I want them to always be strong. Umm the strength... just keep praying to God, e'ery day. Umm for me I don't know. My kids is my strength. Umm this situation that I am most definitely made me open my eyes and realize that umm... nobody is going to do anything for me but myself... So. It's some lovin' people around me, don't get me wrong. But I feel like, I jus need to be alone and do things for me and my kids. Being a adult will coss you a lot of work. Adulting is hard. Yes, too harsh, but I mean I don't let that break me down 'er...you know. It's just the situation that I was in prior to, being homeless, that can... that caused a lot of reflection on the things that I'm feeling now. So, basically I'm taking it step by step and building myself back up. Having low self-esteem, having...not being happy, sad all the time, depressed all the time. That all played a role in where I am now.

Umm, jus focus on the thing that you got going on like, me being homeless I'm focusing on like getting everything together like paperwork, umm every documentation that they need, and be patient. I mean patient will get you a long way, too. That's the only thing. Life in a shelter is not different, it's flustratin'. It's very flustratin' to where you can't find nowhere for you and your kids to go, or stay, or budget the pricing. It's flustratin', it's depressin'. And sometimes you be wantin' to give up, but you... you have to keep on keep on pushing and keep on pushing. So like, the price range is really where it's at. Like its houses to where they have rent 13, 14, 15 hundred dollars. And sometime you have these landlords to where they want you to make three times the rent. So, and den say for instance we don't have housing programs, section 8 anything like that. How would we be able to get out here, when we don't have a certain babysitter or anything to watch our kids to get this job, to sacrifice for us to pay rent. What would it be the next option for us? Back homeless. You can't afford the water bill, you can't afford the light bill. It need to be more resources out here in order for us people that can't provide for ourselves, basically. The resources may already exist, but it's always no funding. They holler it's no funding. Or they don't ecept section 8, or these other programs that I'm connected to through the shelter. It's still a hard time trying to get a house cuz it's none available. They need to build more houses, they need to build more apartments. But ya can't do that if you ain't got no fundin'. It's jus hard out here. It's hard, and... I donno, it's jus hard.

Before they give us that list to call on, they need ta make sure that they call the landlords before we get turnt down, or disappointed, or dismiss. They need to make sure that these are the landlords that ecept this program. This the landlord that ecept section 8, instead of us gettin' on our phones calling dem and getting' turnt down. Ya'll should know this before you even hand out the call list to anyone cuz ya already knew they wouldn't have housing, instead of telling us to keep calling around. For what? To keep getting' denied? To keep getting' turnt down? And den yall give us a certain time to be out da shelter. How do you give a set date to be out when we have nowhere to go? It's people out here with income that's still strugglin'. That still can't afford to pay rent, utilities, food, water. We have 30-60 days to find housing, but sometimes the professionals cancel at the last minute or don't show up for appointments, so we be sitting here for weeks and weeks again, waiting for someone to come talk to us. Even when you find a house, if the house needs inspection you have to wait a month until they do the inspection. I mean, what's the point of the programs when it's no help. At this point, I don't want no program no more. I don't. Like, I jus wanna get a job and be on my own.

Burn After Reading

An anonymous story as told to Brandy Flack

Please don't use my name. I'm surprised I even got up and said I'll talk about being here. I'm more of a laid-back, quiet person, a sit-back-and-observe-type person. I don't just jump into it. But it was something to do, so I figured I'd go ahead and talk. But I shocked myself. I don't want my name on anything, though.

This is the first time we been in this situation. I have a 13-year-old and 4-year-old. We been here at the shelter almost three months. It's hard, the way people treat you when you don't have a home. They treat you like a rag on the floor. Why? I think they do it because they feel like they have a power over us. That's what I've always said, they look down on us because we're here. But some people are only a paycheck away from being here. A lot of the people who treat us bad might not have that much more than us, other than a roof over their heads. And they might be one bad thing from being in the same situation here.

Back when I came here – my car was taken from me, got repoed or something. And I was doing Instacart, grocery shopping and delivery for people. And with me losing my car, of course, that's how I worked, so I couldn't do that anymore. And then I tried to get rental assistance, but I had to wait a long time because there's so many people waiting for a caseworker. So, we got evicted and had to come here. It *is* somewhere to lay your head and not be out in the streets, but it's not the best living situation.

My daughter cried when we first came here. After we were put out, we had stayed in a hotel and spent, like, $300 just for three days. It adds up. So, after a few days I couldn't do it no more and we had to come here. I mean the hotel was nice; we could eat when we wanted and wake up when we wanted to. That's a good thing about it, but it's very costly. So, now we have to stay here.

Before we came here, we lived out in the suburbs and my daughter still goes to school out there. Her dad drives here and picks her up every day, takes her to school, then goes back to the school to pick her up and bring her back here to the shelter. I'm trying to get a place back there. If I tell the school about this now, they'll kick her out. It makes me nervous. I been hoping we can just finish this school year out and if I have to do open enrollment for next year, I will. I just get scared. Hopefully, we could live in the same area again, and then we won't have to worry about it. I'll just give them my new address.

Me and her dad have a good relationship. If it wasn't for him, we couldn't do it. I mean, of course he doesn't like we're in this situation, but he's not in a position to help. And we could stay with him, but I'd rather have my own place because if I go stay with somebody else, I'm still in the same situation. I still don't have my own place. I'd rather come here and get us a place, get established. I don't wanna have to live with somebody else.

We were here for Thanksgiving, but my 13-year-old was lucky enough to get to go out of town. I was supposed to go too but of course I couldn't afford it. But me and my younger one, my son, went over to their dad's house for the holiday for like two nights so we didn't have to be here. That was nice. And we ended up losing our bed here when we left. They want you to check in by like 5:30 and if you're not here for check-in, they give it away. There's a lot of people who need somewhere to stay these days.

I have high blood pressure, and I hadn't had pills in a while, so being here is kind of a good thing. To be able to see a doctor. And I've built a couple good relationships here. I have three main families you'll see me with every day. We share things, our kids play. They go back and forth like sisters. None of my daughter's friends know. She has a lot of friends at school. She's been at her school pretty much since kindergarten. A couple of her friends have asked her to come over, and she always says no. She makes up excuses. She says she's going to her granny's house or something that sounds real.

I miss cooking. The food. I miss the peace and quiet. I miss getting up when I want to, doing stuff whenever I want to. I have all our stuff in storage. I have to try to keep it. Everything we own is in there. If they take that, then we're really gonna be in a worse situation. It's all we have left. So like I say, it's not an ideal situation here. I mean, it's not terrible like a nightmare, but in the same breath it's not good neither.

My mom and my grandmother are still around here where I grew up. I do have a good relationship with my mom. I mean, we talk, but she doesn't know we're here. I didn't tell her. The only people who know we're here are two of my close friends and then my sister. And then of course their dad. But I didn't tell my mom. I didn't want to tell her and then she'll, like, tell the whole family. We usually talk once a day, but sometimes when she calls, I'll go in the bathroom and close the door and talk to her. I don't want her to know where we're at. She still thinks we're in our last house. I just don't tell people. I don't want everyone to know my business. Like I tell their dad, don't tell nobody. If I want the person to know something, I'll tell 'em myself.

I was hoping maybe we could be out of here before Christmas. I would at least like to be able to be in a house and put a tree up. I'm not gonna say it can't happen, but it's hard to try to find places that will work with the housing program, especially trying to live in the suburbs. It's hard. I hope we can. I don't know what Christmas looks like here. We're not gonna stay here on Christmas Eve, though. If I have to get some money and we stay in a hotel Christmas-Eve night, we're not gonna be here.

So, that's where my mind is now.

Not a Superhero, But

An anonymous story as told to Lee Teevan

Our force field needs repair.

Our protective shield has been scratched up recently, but I am doing what I can to fix it for my three kids and me.

At this moment, we are huddled together in this ear-shattering, sometimes dangerous shelter, but my kids and I are calm and they're happy. This moment is a stepping stone to a better tomorrow.

I'm a survivor. I am 25 and for the past four years, I've lived with intimate partner violence.

No more.

Somehow in the insanity that followed the very last time my ex abused me, I got the blame. Although I called the police on him for hitting me, I was the one who sat in jail, away from my kids, for a week.

The first crack in our shield: I got arrested.

The fractures continued: I lost my full-time job and my apartment.

The major assault: My ex's mom called CPS on me for neglecting my children and I lost them for a week.

I emerged from a week of jail with solutions. I went back to my job and explained what happened. I got my old job back.

I got my three kids back and they're safe, healthy, and happy. I love my kids and I've got to stay grounded and focused. They are my center, my meaning, my loves.

Their lives will be different from mine.

When I was four, the age of my oldest, I remember my little brother and me being hungry. Mom fed us cold leftover spaghetti, but my senses were overpowered by the rich aroma of warm fresh Chinese food she and her boyfriend-of-the-moment were eating.

My children will never inhale that stench of disregard and neglect.

I put them first. See how they laugh and run into my arms? That never happened with my mom.

I still see my mom. In fact, we work together. We pass each other in the hallways, never saying a word to one another. No one knows that we are mother and daughter. The only time she speaks to me is when she asks for money. I have given her some in the past, but no more. My kids are my focus.

I'm getting to know my father. He was in prison for much of my childhood. Now he's out, but his health is terrible, and I can't see him very much.

My ex and I are finished, but I want my kids to have a good relationship with him. Right now, he doesn't want them around. If he has them, he'll call me, "They're out of diapers. I'm dropping them off at your place." I gave him $300 in food stamps before I went to jail. He still complained about buying them food and diapers.

Things are going to change soon. I am going to ask for child support and get his name on our kids' birth certificates. He will have to get a job and start providing for the three children he fathered.

I am laser-focused on my kids.

I am on my own and I'm going to figure it out. I love my kids and I have got to stay positive for them.

I've got a job. I am going to work with a housing program to get my family into a permanent home. I contacted the local community college today to figure out how to get my GED and start college. I am going to get my driver's license.

I am no superhero, but I am a very strong woman whose superpower is my love for my kids.

Nothing's going to hurt that force field.

Section 2: Discussion Questions

We want to thank the various shelters and organizations in Dayton that supported this project. These organizations and their staff work 24 hours a day to help shelter and provide services to those experiencing homelessness. Numerous people are supported and helped by these organizations each year. Unfortunately, for many, living on the streets or in cars is a very traumatic experience. These stories reflect both the assistance and sometimes the negative experiences of our systems.

1. What story most resonated with you and why?

2. What were some of the reasons people were experiencing homelessness in this section? What surprised you? What are some other reasons that people in our community experience homelessness?

3. What are ways our community attempts to help those experiencing homelessness? What are ways we can better support our shelter systems and unhoused communities?

4. What are some possible ways you could volunteer or donate to help with this crisis in our community?

Resources to learn and read more about the problem of homelessness in the United States (A more detailed resource guide and question guide is provided at the end of this book):

National Coalition for the Homeless: https://nationalhomeless.org/

Coalition on Housing and Homelessness in Ohio https://cohhio.org/

SECTION 3

"**E**viction is a cause, not just a condition, of poverty. No moral code or ethical principle, no piece of scripture, or holy teaching, can be summoned to defend what we have allowed our country to become."

— Matthew Desmond

These stories are the lived experiences of those who lost their housing either through eviction or other circumstances. Most in this section are now housed and living their lives. However, they still remember their stories and wanted to share them for others to understand.

Stories About Eviction and Housing Insecurity

Because of This Number

An anonymous poem as told to Amanda Hayden

Because of this number
    I have thousands of photographs now
printed and stored
along with the sweet, tiny outfits
my kids wore home
after they were born
also, baby teeth, science projects,
trophies, report cards, ribbons
every report progress card
boxes and boxes of memories
Because of this number
I could never paint my room as a kid
could never exhale fully
could never settle in

I learned to never get too comfortable
security was a mocking illusion
home was just a color here
a flash there, a ripped couch
stuffing stuck in mid escape
the dresser I liked that one day disappeared
just a temporary place
with a scratched coffee table
tv trays, a stitched
phantom Frankenstein
it all blurs together
but I was one of the lucky ones
because I had grandparents
ones who gave me envelopes
that turned into a lunch
or a pair of pants
or an unscarred holiday memory
theirs the only address that ever stayed put
as I passed through 29 houses by the age of 30
Because of this number
so many things were lost, but never my grit
no matter which school, classroom
or desk I was placed in
I grabbed my pencil
education my lifeline, my only constant
my rope pulling me out of this hopeless abyss
Because of this number
I raised children who are

cradled in their home's arms
a home that is warm
with an address that stays
a home that is not
a phantom or blur
Because of this number
Despite this number
I found my way out
I found my way out

Listening to Children

Anonymous stories as told to Kathy Rowell

"Children are the living messages we send to a time we will not see."
— Neil Postman

This story is being shared as part of a research project conducted by Professor Kathy Rowell, Sociologist, Sinclair Community College. During January through April 2022, she had the opportunity to interview 24 children ages 8 to 13 about their experiences with housing insecurity (all the children had experienced eviction and/or homelessness. Some were in shelters or living in difficult circumstances during the interview). Both parents and the children gave permission for their words to be used in publication. To protect anonymity, the names, locations, and ages are not being shared. It is estimated that children experience housing insecurity and eviction more than any other demographic group in the United States. Facing homelessness and eviction is traumatic for children and thus questions were asked in such a way to reduce trauma and give children agency in deciding what they wanted to share with the interviewer.

These are their exact quotes and words as shared with me during the project.

What does "rent" mean to you?

Oh, you're not buying a house but you're just like you're renting it.

You're not buying the house, but you're just living in it for a while.

It means that you are getting money. It has something to do with bills or something like that.

So, you know when you get a house, you gotta pay to stay there. Like you gotta pay for your water bill.

You have a house and if you want to keep it you have to pay to live in it.

It means you have to pay the landlord.

It means to pay someone to live in a place. Okay. Or, to like, like, use a vehicle for a period of time.

Like when you borrow a car or something? And then once you're done with it, you give it back?

Rent is like when you rent something like your house or car

You got to get a certain amount of money to stay in a house.

It is what you pay for your house.

Paying bills and stuff.

Umm there is a lot of stuff like rent to own. It is hard to explain.

You put money into a bank account.

We pay half or something for a house, not like the full payment. You're just paying because you're staying there. If you want to buy it then you have to pay like full amount.

It means when you have to pay to live somewhere.

What is a landlord?

Landlord means the person that has the house that takes to make sure the house is good.

There's somebody that owns the house, and that inspects the house to make sure you to take care of it.

I am not speaking about that because I am not sure. I think it has something to do with owning a home or something.

They kicked me out of my home. This is why I am here in the shelter.

He comes to check your house and get the rent money so we will stay in the house. He lends the house to you.

It is the person you buy the house from.

They let you stay in the house if you pay them.

Oh, everyone is someone that owns a house that sells to you to use.

Something that like, helps you with your house. And like, clean it.

Somebody's who is like, if you don't pay your bills like they will kick you out. It is like you got a loan and you don't pay your bills and they kick you out.

People that come in, like, collect your money and stuff like that. To make sure people have money, so you won't say you want to get out, get put out to a house and stuff like.

They are the people you buy your house from. You pay them rent.

You give them money to pay your bills.

But if you don't own it, you pay it to a landlord that is not yourself.

They rent house and they buy and sell houses.

The landlord keep in charge of the house and come check on it and see if it's clean. So don't anybody get kicked out the houses.

They own the houses and they make sure that houses is clean and stuff.

A landlord build the house like they buy houses that's been abandoned for many year. And they fix them up and like start selling them for people and then that's how they make money from the people renting.

Yes, we have had a lot of landlords. They made sure like your house is like stable and like you need something they're like come in and fix it. Okay, like they inspect your house or something.

What do you think of landlords?

She will be nice to me.

They are mostly good but can be mean sometimes.

They look at people's houses to see if they are clean. That is what my old landlord did. They came every month to see if our house was clean.

Some are nice and some are mean.

I don't like landlords. I just wanna live in our own house we don't have to pay money to live in it. So can live in for free.

Landlords are kind of mean. They are not fair. They kicked us out of our house for no reason.

Some could be assholes. Some can't.

I don't like when they kick people out and people been say that they've been trying. Because they really been trying and some people don't have enough money because they've been going through stuff.

I just wish they could do their job more like answer the phone and fix stuff. You know how people be talking how the landlord don't answer their phone and don't fix stuff around the house.

I have never met a landlord but the way they treated us wasn't right. I don't like how they talked to my mom.

They should help the poor more.

What does "eviction" mean?

Eviction means you got like kicked out of the house and you can't come...you can't come back to it.

Eviction means that you got kicked out the house because you didn't pay your rent.

I haven't learned that word yet because I failed third grade due to COVID19. I hated it but I love school.

It means when you like have to go to court. It is like when you get on the streets. And you get on the streets and nobody cares. They call you gross and stuff and they never care. And you ask them for charity and they'll won't to come near you. Oh man, they be mean. They admit they was in your shoes. They will be sorry for you.

You get put out of your house. I don't know why you get put out but you do.

When people get kicked out for not following rules.

Eviction is like, if this house was dirty, and like that, there was lots of holes in the wall (points to hole in the wall). We could end up getting evicted because we've not taken care of the house.

It is like you did something bad or something.

It means you have to leave a place you live because you can't pay rent or maybe you were too messy or there was a lot of commotion going on in the building.

Do you know anyone who has ever been evicted?

Yes, us by our landlord.

I'm pretty sure my stepdad got evicted for theft.

I have been watching this show and it makes me cry. People get a little bit stuck and they need help and no one helps. Like there was this girl and her mom looking for empty bottles to recycle for money. But yeah, this man, he had an empty bottle and saw the girl looking for bottles, but threw in the trash right in front of her and said, get it yourself you stinky little rat.

Ya a cousin got kicked out because he was playing loud music or something like that. People made noise complaints.

Yes, we have been kicked out a few times.

What does homelessness mean?

It means to have no job.

You are on the streets and you have covers and you lay on the ground.

It means you are on the streets. You got no food, no money, no place to live.

It means you don't have no house, you don't live nowhere. No food.

You're on the street and you ask them for money, they fail to help you. It's like, just like a slave. But it different. It's just like a slave but it's different.

You stand on the corner and you choose not to go to school or get a job.

Being homeless is a bad thing. It is a sad thing. People be down on their luck.

Homeless means you are having the worst day. You are on the streets.

Poor living outside. Don't have no home. Don't have no food.

You don't have money or something. You are hungry.

You don't have a home.

You have no place to live.

Do you know anyone who has been homeless?

Yes, I think we are homeless because this place is called a homeless shelter. But we are getting a house soon so we will not be homeless anymore.

I saw these peoples in the roads. Sometimes I see homeless pets. It is sad. I saw a baby kitten that was homeless. I have seen homeless pets.

Of course, yeah. My Dad was homeless but he has a house now.

Us.

Me. Because we don't have a house.

A couple of my mom's friends are homeless.

It is just like I explained with eviction. It is like eviction but a little different. You on the streets. I have seen people on the streets.

I do know some homeless people, but I don't know their names.

I have seen them walking around the streets and stuff.

Like a couple, I don't know. But every time I see homeless people, I give stuff to them. One day I went with my Dad to buy stuff to help people who don't have enough to eat. I give people my stuff because they are homeless and don't have enough to eat. They are like my brothers and sisters too!

My dad and me.

I do, but I don't know all their names yet.

Yes, my cousins.

I think my best friend in school was homeless. She missed school because her mom was in jail and she had no place to live.

What does it mean to have a house?

It is exciting. You have your own room, your own bed to sleep in. You have your own "peace." You can watch TV.

You will have your own TV, your own personal space whenever you want. Chilling your own bed. You can eat whenever, you go to sleep whenever you want. You won't have to worry about knowing you want to play with somebody.

It means fun. You can go to sleep when you want to. Watch TV if you want to.

You have to go through all these really hard things like you have to pay the water bill, the electricity bill and you have to like, make sure you don't spend too much also you won't have enough money to spend it on food and stuff.

And like, it's like a comfortable bed that you could say *boy, that's nice*. I like comfortable beds. My favorite place was probably the place that I live, like, around the corner from my dad's house. That'd be nice. I could always walk to his house or ride my bike.

You have your own space and privacy. I liked the house we had that had four bedrooms. I liked having my own bedroom.

It's like, it's like a good thing that you live in and you sleep in your beds that have peaceful nights and stuff. And when you will leave you have to lock your doors or someone will break in your house and into all your stuff. So you have to always lock your doors. But make sure you always have a key for your door. We get to turn the heat on when it gets cold. And I like my mom's comfortable bed.

It means you got a roof over your head and a place to sleep.

It means you have somewhere to lay your head and get to be with your family and have family support.

I don't know because I have never really lived in my own home before.

I feel grateful when I have my own home. I don't like sleeping at other people's places. You know what I mean? I feel weird. But I wouldn't want to sleep on the street either.

It feels good to have my own place. Really good.

It is good to have it and be thankful for it. And to not have that nasty food that is in the shelter anymore.

You got more room, and you don't got to worry about anything.

You got a PS4, you can have a guinea pig, and a car.

It feels good because I can have more animals.

What do you think grownups can do to help kids so they don't have to be evicted, homeless or poor?

I would just like to feel better. I am tired of feeling sick. I also just want kids to stop bullying me. I just want people to be nice to me.

Help people get off the streets like giving them shelter. Give people blankets, shelter, money and food.

Take them to the store and buy them some things and just help them.

Give them some money like $25 or $100 bill so they can buy some clothes or food in the house. And give them vitamins and food. Help by investing in and helping kids grow. Try to help them keep their home. Help them keep their home, yeah help them build or buy a home.

Nobody should be homeless. Get everybody a house.

Make good food for people. Help at shelters. Be careful with kids and try to help them.

Give them more attention. They could give them candy and make them more happy.

I think some kids could go to an orphanage or get adopted or just give some families money and help them.

They should give them money and stuff.

Try to help them out early and get them back on the feet, stuff like that. Start a community.

Donate money.

Start a group home and make a shelter.

Make it more better for kids. Have food for kids and beds for kids. And have more room for kids.

I would tell grownups like make sure the shelter is way better for kids and to just make it more kiddish. Like the one downtown they need to make it more kiddish. The only thing you can have in your room is water. You can't bring any snacks. Make the shelter more kiddish, it felt like a jail. I would make it more comfortable so people felt like they were in a home.

Better food at the shelter, better toys. Make the outside nicer. Make the learning center downstairs okay. There was this lady and she was eating chips in front of me and getting it on my papers. It was gross. Make the learning center downstairs nicer.

I would tell them to get rid of the Coronavirus. I think it would be nice to have animals at the shelter. Animals are nice. I would like healthy food.

Don't cuss or fight in front of them.

What would your dream home be like?

I would like a mansion. I want my own PC and room. I want to be a gamer when I grow up.

I would like to live on a farm. I think it would be fun.

I would like to live in a fortune house. Almost fill the whole world up. A big house. All the way up to the sun. Like past one cloud. You could see everything, and I would love it. I would just live in it and nobody else. I would have a playroom and everything. I would have anything I want. I am very rich and I could get anything I want.

A mansion bigger than this place (the shelter).

A mansion with 6 rooms. 12 bathrooms.

A cottage in the middle of nowhere with no annoying neighbors.

I want a mansion. Really big. And like a big pool and a backyard. And a water slide.

My dream house will be like big but not too big.

A ten-story mansion but it would be hard to walk up 10 steps.

A four-bedroom house for me, my brothers and mom to be together.

Really big with a swimming pool and a lot of rooms. I want a lot of rooms so people can be with me.

A big mansion with a gym like a fitness center and a bowling alley.

Gold everywhere with a big heart of gold in the middle for my mom. And a car for my mom.

Having all my family together in a big building.

A four-story house with an elevator. With a pool outside and a spa for my mom. I would make it really big so it could also be an orphanage to help kids.

A two-story house with 4 bedrooms and three bathrooms and a guinea pig and PS4.

I would like to have a washer and dryer. I would like to have a space for a garden and plants to grow my own food. I like plants.

I imagine a big mansion with 13 rooms, 10 bathrooms, two pools, two jacuzzis, areas where you might be alone or like family time. I want a big house. I have seen them on tv shows and they look fine. You can have a lot of people live with you and have a lot of stuff.

I want a place where I can have a zoo in the backyard.

No Sense of Humanity

An anonymous story as told to Jenna Beck

The lights around me flared to life and a quiet night was pierced by the screams of a raving woman.

I looked around and realized that I was still on the floor of the shelter's bathroom. I had been sleeping. *We* had been sleeping, my two young daughters, Sophia and Selena, resting on top of me. We were awoken by screams and a loud pounding on the bathroom door. It was jarring, especially for my daughter Sophia. She's autistic and requires quiet to allow her little body to fully rest. At this shelter, the only place that afforded us that quiet is the bathroom floor. It was not ideal, but it was our only option. The shelter's open sleeping room was filled with fifty, maybe sixty people all making their own noises and movements. Our van was usually an option, but it was below freezing that night, and I had very little gas. So, the bathroom floor it was. Even though I could not control much of my life during this time, my children were, and still remain, my top priority.

When I finally became conscious enough to understand what was going on, I realized the woman screaming at me was accusing me of using drugs in the bathroom. I am infuriated by this accusation. I am furious, and I am just so incredibly exhausted.

A lot of people think that people who are homeless have a place to go. The reality is that if there is no one who wants you, there is nowhere to go.

Trust me when I say that I would have rather been anywhere but that bathroom floor. I had to move my daughters three times, and this was by far the worst shelter my girls and I had been in. So many of the people who worked there did not even treat you like a human. The lights turned off at 7:00 no matter what, sometimes even earlier if the employees were having a bad day. I had to shower in the dark and get myself and my children dressed in the dark. And even though we were in the middle of a pandemic, nothing was cleaned well. At one point, the beds we had been sleeping on were previously occupied by a family with COVID, and there had been no sterilization. While meals were served here, we went many nights without food. Eating in a large noisy cafeteria was impossible for Sophia to manage, so I scrounged up any food I could, and we ate in our car. The shelter refused to give us food or allow us to sit somewhere quiet so she would not have to suffer from sensory overload. When shelter employees attempted to help and give us food to take to our van, they got in trouble. There was never any compassion for us or Sophia's needs.

Even just getting into this shelter required a wait in a long line. Both girls struggled waiting, and they did not understand why we were here or why we kept moving from place to place. How could I explain this all to them? How could I tell them that their father is a drug dealer or that he tried to kill me on more than one occasion? You cannot turn to a child who is autistic and tell them, "I'm sorry. We have no place else to go." She wouldn't understand, and at the end of the day maybe I do not even understand why we found ourselves here. It was all something I never imagined for myself. When you marry someone, you are in love, and you are happy. You do not see red flags. You ignore them. There is an in-love barrier. I've tried to hide and run so much it's exhausting. I never asked to be homeless, and this is not what I wanted for my girls. I have changed so much about myself in an attempt to keep us safe. The only thing I have left is my personality, and my personality is what has kept us alive.

Reading this, it might seem like a woman screaming at me in a bathroom pales in comparison to what I have otherwise endured. I have been strangled, hit, pushed, and beaten to within an inch of my life. I have had to meticulously plan an escape from my abuser in hopes of avoiding a repeat experience. I have had to do all of this with two young girls in my care. But difficulties do not exist in a vacuum. They build and, in our case, dehumanize us. So when an angry woman stood outside the shelter's bathroom door and started screaming her assumptions, it ripped apart the last shreds of my humanity. In her head, I was being painted with a brush over which I had no control. She had forgotten that I was a woman with a story, history, and personality. If any part of this story resonates with you, let it be this: treat those who are homeless with compassion. We did not choose this. No one ever would.

The screaming woman called the police to come to the bathroom. I was left sitting there, holding my daughters, clinging to the last semblance of my pride. There are no words to describe how her accusations made me feel. An officer came, but thankfully, he knew me and my girls. He was aware of Sophia's situation. He knew we were humans and not caricatures made up in the mind of a screaming woman. He vouched for me that I would never do what she was accusing me of.

The situation passed. No apology from the woman. No peaceful sleep for my girls. No sense of humanity for me.

Eviction Was the Best Thing for My Family

An anonymous story as told to Melanie Cooper

When you hear eviction, it usually brings uncertainty and sadness. The stories you hear are heartbreaking and at times start a cycle of events that seem to just keep you in a struggling situation. But my story is different. My story of eviction is one that brought a much-needed change that turned out to be the best thing for my family and me.

The summer before I started high school, I was living with my parents and my younger brother. He's like two years younger than me. I had lived in the house for as long as I remember. We lived on the east side of Dayton, on Patterson (the "white" side of town). It was my grandmother's house. She rented it to us. I think what happened was my dad lost his job, and my parents were late with rent for a couple of months. So, she evicted us. I know! Crazy to think my grandmother evicted us; how can you evict your own family out of the house they are staying at? Especially when they are struggling and going through a hard time.

My relationship with my grandmother (she was white) never really existed. She never really approved of my parents' relationship. My mom is white and my dad's Black. She was racist. I think she was waiting for something to happen, an excuse so she could get us to leave. I don't remember being sad about it. I never really liked the house; it was like it had bad vibes. I mean, I don't know if that was because it was my grandmother's house; but I was just not attached to it even though I lived there most of my life, at least as long as I remember.

Going to school there on the east side was hard. I went to mostly white schools, and it was weird since I didn't grow up in white culture because I didn't have contact with my mother's side of the family. I was closer to my dad's side of the family. So, though I went to schools that were predominantly white, I was raised in Black culture. We spent holidays with my dad's huge extended family, all my cousins, aunts, and uncles. I knew I was racially mixed, but never identified with being white or what it meant to be white in America. I love Black culture, the music—food like my Black grandmother's cooking.

So, when I moved to the west side of Dayton, I stayed on the predominantly Black side of town. When we moved, I thought it was great. I was like, why is anyone sad? My dad got a new job, a better job, and he enjoyed what he was doing, too. He also started to study and get different tech certificates. He works in IT and was advancing and pursuing his dreams career-wise. So, even though the house on the west side was a little bit more expensive, my parents could afford it because he was advancing in his career.

And the new house was beautiful, way better than the one before. It was a historic house with beautiful hardwood floors. I had a huge room. It had a huge backyard and kitchen. I spent four years there, my whole time in high school and my freshman year of college.

Then later on my parents were able to buy their first house. It was farther west. I don't like it as much because we are so far removed from everything since we are in the suburbs. But this was a huge step for my parents; they are building generational wealth.

So, even though this is not your usual story about eviction, it just shows that sometimes things we experience that may seem challenging or detrimental can be the opening of a new and better journey or opportunities. It can even become an improvement in your life.

She's Covered

D's story as told to Jamie Gee

Granny has been gone just over a year, but it feels like I lost her a year and a half ago. I truly miss her beyond measure and pray my silent grief leads to a waterfall of forgiveness one day. She was a beautiful soul who moved with such strength and tenacity. She covered everyone in her circle of influence, including me. Born in Kentucky with fourteen siblings, she always made a way out of no way, making sure we were okay until she wasn't. I knew Granny was dying of cancer, and the layered stress of dealing with a possible eviction was added weight to diminishing health.

In early fall, she called me because she'd received a housing violation notification placed on her door implying somebody lived there, that wasn't supposed to be there. As soon as I got off work, I made a special trip to her home to read the violation for myself. As I watched Granny holding her forehead in disbelief, it was evident she was confused and troubled with understanding why this was happening to her.

As a senior citizen living in her apartment home complex for 15 years, she had never had an incident or missed a payment. My mother had been there for a long time, taking care of Granny through her chronic illness. So, I knew she felt helpless. I immediately did what I could to contact the apartment manager and see what had occurred. The onsite Manager was nonchalant at best and said the person who was responsible for the notice was based out of the State of Florida and that was the only way we could get to the bottom of the matter. Absolutely no information was provided about the person they claimed was living at Granny's house, so that's when we went directly to the Sheriff's Office in Englewood. We wanted answers, and to save her from heartache and trouble.

Once I got to the Sheriff's office, my son at my side, I began expressing my inquiries about Granny's notice. They told us it was my cousin who reported he lived at her apartment upon his release from prison, which was the furthest from the truth. According to the local Sheriff's office, we were advised he was not allowed to be in the Englewood area or any address at the apartment complex due to his eviction violation, which was the reason she had received a citation. My anger turned to resentment.

It wasn't too much longer after Granny received the second notice that I contacted the Office of Reentry for intervention to locate any resources for legal help. Imagine the relief I felt when it was confirmed her address was not my cousin's approved residence per the parole office. That day, several attempts were made to report this finding by contacting the property owner in Florida, to no avail. Listening to the ongoing prompts to reach a live person when you're in crisis is no fun. However, stumbling upon pre-recorded voice prompts to connect with a "legal liaison" provided a ray of hope until selecting the prompt with anticipation, resulting in yet another voicemail. Multiple messages were left that day for the company headquarters which landed on deaf ears for three weeks. The longest three weeks of my life.

During that time, my hopelessness increased, and faith decreased, and I questioned my ability to aid her at that moment. All I could think of was how she unselfishly covered me. *My Granny was my "rock." She was my hero. The one who raised me.* So, for me not to be able to handle this situation and find a resolution for her made me feel helpless. I knew I couldn't give up without a fight. So, in the midst of that, I contacted legal aid and completed an online application, and spoke with Miami Valley Fair Housing about the situation to see what I could do from there.

By that time my grandmother was in and out of the hospital, and in and out of nursing homes due to her illness. She was battling cancer, so she couldn't provide a good fight. My focus shifted. Every day before going to work, I would visit her at Miami Valley Hospital from around 4:30 to 5 in the morning, and I had to be at work by 7:30. As I operated in survival mode, the apartment headquarters in Florida finally returned my call, yet a call too late. Within two weeks the third notice of eviction arrived, and time had run out. She had to be out of the apartment, and I knew at that moment I was called to advocate for her. When I entered the Vandalia courtroom for the eviction hearing on her behalf that day, I didn't know what to expect. I was advised I couldn't speak for her because I wasn't a lawyer.

The Judge did not understand my role initially until I told him my grandmother was gravely ill and she couldn't be there. Once the judge allowed me to talk, I told him she was battling cancer and had been in and out of the hospital and nursing home, and he finally allowed me to take the stand. As I took the stand, I became Granny's soldier. At that moment I felt I had to fight for my grandmother because she couldn't fight for herself. I then explained the details of what happened, and that Granny had done no wrong; but her grandson had reported her address as his proposed reentry residence, which had been subsequently denied by the parole office. In conclusion, the judge told me to bring back the paperwork to support Granny's medical condition, and the information on her grandson, and he set a court date for me to return with the documents in hand.

I reported for the second scheduled hearing in November 2021 and provided the Judge with the documents he looked over. His decision confirmed we still needed to evacuate her apartment, but that she would not get fined for the property owner's claim. Granny passed on December 3rd, 2021 . . . three weeks after her 77th birthday.

Feelings of sorrow, anger, numbness, bitterness, and emptiness took my mind over, and I was emotionally unavailable to everyone, including myself. Looking back on Granny's eviction process, I really felt like dying inside. My grandmother wasn't there to fight for herself. She wasn't in her right mind, and I was trying to do the best I could to help and appeared to be failing her. She had given everybody life, but we ultimately had to put our house, and her to rest. I felt that the system was broken, and it failed her, and it broke me at the same time.

Granny is the one who raised me, so I called her "Mom." We used to enjoy shopping and watching movies together and seeing her bowl put a smile on my face. She lived up to her nickname "Miss Jazzy" and loved listening to Temptations music around the Christmas holidays, the best time of the year. The first Christmas without her felt empty.

Something was missing, a "hole" and void we couldn't fill. When she passed, our sense of fellowship surrounding the most wonderful time of the year began to fade.

My grandmother used to tell me, "With your mouth, you should be able to do anything," and "You talk too much, and you think you know everything." She spoke my qualities into existence, and I landed in a career of advocating and helping others. I am always trying to save everybody.

P.S. Granny – Although I could not save you from this situation, I've found comfort in knowing I covered you. Thank you for all you have done. Thank you for the life and legacy you have left for us. I thought you'd like to know your grandson apologized. I'm still missing your home-cooked meals made from almost barren cabinets. Just know your favorite dressing recipe is in good hands. Save some beans and cornbread for me.

Love, D

19 Times

Mindy Parade's story as told to Kathleen Gish

Since you asked, I added it up. I had never counted it before. I've moved at least nineteen times. I am fairly sure that number is higher, but I cannot put my finger on what I'm forgetting. There weren't nineteen places. I moved back in with my grandma at least three times. But, it felt a little bit different each time because of the rotating cast of characters squatting at her home at any given time. This included my father, who was *not* her son, and no longer married to her daughter. I called him James.

To accurately capture my grandmother's house, picture a crash pad for unemployed alcoholics—*not* a place to dry—and then add in a boarding house for grandchildren whose parents no longer wanted them. This is where I grew up. The thing is, I did not realize this was problematic until fairly recently. I mean, when all you know is instability, it feels normal.

When I was little, I smelled like pee and cigarettes. I didn't know other people didn't smell like pee and cigarettes. One of my teachers bought me a pair of shoes once, because mine were in such bad shape. I was the kid that schools collected used coats for. They pulled us out of class to have us pick one. I realized I was embarrassed. I was *supposed* to be embarrassed.

There are so many things that exist just to make sure poor people perform their shame. Shaming rituals, if you will. Take the job center. It is set up in a way that no matter how well prepared you are, you are found lacking. You are in the wrong line, even though that other lady told you to get into this line. You never have the right documents, even if you bring every scrap of paper that has ever been relevant to your life. It is on purpose, too, to make sure we don't forget that we are inadequate. The whole system is like a mother telling you, "You should be ashamed of yourself!"

Sometimes you can't help but revel in the farce. One year, I got a letter from the IRS saying someone else had already used my son's social security number and claimed him as a dependent. To remedy the situation, I was told to send in evidence that he was really my son. What does that even mean? I sent in copies of all his documents, birth certificate, and social security card. They sent me another letter. I somehow had not met their burden of proof. So, I took my birthing video, burnt it to a disc, and wrote "Documentation" on it. I sent that in with the next bundle of paperwork.

I've owned a house before. Two in fact. I treated them like I treated rentals. They were temporary. I did not see them as investments. When things broke, I worked around them. If a pipe burst, I fixed it with duct tape. Chaos was normal. I sold my first house when I split up with my boyfriend at the time. I moved out of the second house before they could foreclose. I did a deed in lieu. I have never actually gotten evicted. You can't get evicted if you leave before they kick you out. It seemed logical to avoid the formalities. Plus, when you are poor, you sort of always expect the bottom to fall out. You are used to "officials" being out to catch you, not out to help you.

I was fifteen when I left high school. They said if my mom signed the form, I could stop coming to school. I didn't want to be there and they didn't want me there. My mom didn't care. Which was why going to college this last time was such a change for me. I had to shift my mindset. I had to at least tell myself that I belonged there, and that everyone wasn't just waiting for a chance to kick me out. I ended up getting an MBA, can you believe it? I had to fight the idea that I was an imposter every step of the way, even when I was learning Latin—seriously, *Latin*, the language—and writing better papers than everyone else in my classes, according to my instructors. My teachers repeatedly told me that. It's like they knew I didn't feel like I belonged, so they needed to convince me I did. Don't take this as bragging, though. Anyone could have done it if they had the privilege to go to college.

I have a home now. Not a house, a home. When things break, I fix them. Novel idea, huh? I love the phrase, "Throw money at the problem." I can actually do that now. People say that like it's a problem, and I get the sense they have been the ones who have always had money to throw at the problem. We laugh, and feel safe in this house. I let my kids decorate their bedrooms exactly how they want. I keep a lot of food in the house. That might be what security feels like to me, when there is an abundance of food.

You asked if I was mad that my life was so unstable. I don't think I was. Even now, looking back, I don't think I am. I'm really glad I got out of it, though. I remind my kids constantly how good they have it, even if they don't really have the frame of reference to understand. But, I can tell you that it did make me mad that after I lost my house, it sat empty. I mean, couldn't I have just stayed there? Why kick people out just to let it sit vacant? Why don't we give people abandoned houses so they can fix them up and have a place to be, and something to be proud of? It certainly makes more sense than leaving them empty.

I don't like to be hyperbolic about my childhood. I am still adjusting to the idea that it was somehow problematic. I simultaneously feel a vast distance from it, but I also feel like it was so recent. I don't feel at all connected to it, yet at times I feel like it defines me. I know you hate this word, but it feels like it really captures things. I was trash. Shouldn't you only be upset by a word if it is hurtful? So, don't worry, I call myself trash, but in a loving way.

Just Because

An anonymous story as told to Leigh Ann Fulford

You ask me why—
    Will "because" suffice?
Will it satisfy you?
I need no justification to stand here at this moment.
Reciting this poem, in this city, in this state.
I need no papers to tell me I must show proof of my long list of lovers
And as sure as the flowers bloom
The world turns;
And as the days turn to long winter nights.
I wake up again.
Just because.

Losing everything you own puts this frantic emphasis on everything you have left. You really value what you decide to take and keep. My most treasured items are a few photographs I have from my childhood.

They remind of how life was when I was a child. It wasn't a super happy environment or a great upbringing, but like many family photos, they were taken at happy moments or when things seemed happy, like holidays, parties, and big school events. These images capture slivers of what I wish my whole childhood could have been like.

I grew up in a conservative community and struggled in school mostly because of mental health issues brought on by my home life, but also because I knew from an early age that I liked girls. My family was OK with me liking girls because almost everyone in my family is bisexual. My dad is the only one who is straight.

But I always felt different. In elementary school, I would often ask my dad why I couldn't live my life as a boy, and his response was that I was too young to know or understand, that I was too young to make those decisions but that I could when I was older. I didn't even know what being trans was at the time. I just knew I didn't like what other girls liked and I didn't act like other girls acted, even though that doesn't quantify being trans—I just felt different.

In 8th grade, I got on the Internet and discovered *transgender* was a thing. I finally had a name for all those feelings I had been having all those years. Everything clicked—I was not only bisexual, but I was also male.

I decided to talk with my mom first because she is bisexual, and I figured she would be more understanding than my father would be. At first, I thought she understood and accepted me. However, I soon learned that she was respecting me only to my face and would misgender me and be transphobic behind my back.

I ended up being involuntarily outed to my dad, who I didn't think would be supportive because of those things he had told me growing up. He pushed back at first, but eventually he accepted my pronouns and would defend me when people would misgender me. I was surprised about his change of heart, and it was so nice to feel respected and have his support. We don't have a perfect relationship—there are moments when the biases he grew up with come into conversation—but I do my best to correct him. In spite of these disagreements, he respects who I am. My mother on the other hand doesn't respect me because she is convinced that transgender didn't exist "before this age came along," which is ignorant.

My mom didn't have a problem with my bisexuality, but my being trans was outside of her life experience and she had more trouble accepting that. The same thing happened at school. Being queer in our conservative school district was hard at first because I was one of the very first visible "gay" people (I presented as a girl at the time, who was in a relationship with another girl), but eventually, the other kids and staff sort of adapted to that, though reluctantly. When I became one of the first visible transgender kids in high school, that was harder to accept.

I have struggled with depression and mental health my whole life but being outed as trans put a bigger strain on my overall well-being. I am still angry about my high school counselor who outed me as trans to all the other teachers and staff. I didn't ask them to do this, but they did anyway, and I don't know why they did this. I think it might have been to get my teachers to respect my pronouns, but I don't see why they told all the teachers in the school without talking to me about it.

The school's political climate was divided. A lot of the teachers and students were very conservative, but not all. Some counselors and teachers started pushing for things like a gender-neutral bathroom to the school board. Again, I never asked for this. Maybe they did it because they realized that trans kids actually exist in their school, but the request created a huge fight and debate between the teachers. It wasn't that I didn't support gender-neutral bathrooms, but it made my "coming out" more visible to the entire community.

Getting through a school day became very hard. Some teachers who knew I preferred *he/him* pronouns would make a point to call me *she/her* because they didn't believe trans people existed or they were bigoted or whatever their reasons were. They would make it very obvious they were misgendering me and made it a point to call me *she*. And then there were other teachers who would respect me and made no big deal about my pronouns.

Because teachers weren't united in their gendering of me, students were confused. They would stop me after class to ask me why I'm called a boy. When I would explain about being trans, I would get some comments that I am "too pretty to be a boy" and that it is "a waste" for me to transition or be trans in general. I also had to hear all the terrible reasons people didn't want gender-neutral bathrooms. They were pushing back with "straight boys will pose as girls to assault other girls in the bathroom" and the sort of thing you hear bigots say on TV, radio, and social media.

Needless to say, the school's and larger community's response and reaction to my being trans contributed to my depression and mental health struggles from growing up in an abusive household. I was put in an afterschool class to help me with my struggles in showing up to school. However, even in that small classroom with just one teacher, I still heard all the comments. I couldn't get away from the bad things people were saying about people like me. Eventually, this, on top of everything else in my life, got to be too much and I dropped out of high school in 11th grade.

About the time I dropped out of school, our family was evicted from our apartment. Even though eviction wasn't new to me, it was still hard.

I was four years old the first time we were evicted. Our family of five lived in a nice big house in a nice part of town. We had an upper-middle-class kind of life that changed abruptly when my dad lost his job in the 2000s. We had to leave our home and move to a hotel for about two years. Five of us moving from a house where everyone had their own bedroom to a hotel room was very difficult. This new "home" life was stressful on all of us, and as I said before, it made my mental health issues worse.

Even before we were evicted, my parents did not have a healthy relationship. My mother continually berated and cheated on my dad. My siblings and I grew up watching this abuse, as well as being on the receiving end of it, and it had detrimental effects on all of us.

Eventually, after over 20 years of marriage, my parents legally separated. My brother was old enough to just leave by then, so he did. After our second eviction, my sister stayed with our mom in an apartment up north for financial purposes. My dad and I moved out and ended up jumping from one hotel to another. Therefore, my "home life" was not stable when I was outed to the community as trans.

After the separation, I was more of a parent to my dad than he was for me. He just doesn't understand or doesn't want to deal with 20 years of what my mom's constant abuse of him did to his mental health. I ended up moving to Cincinnati with friends for a while and then moved back in with my dad after my friends, and I had a falling out after the pandemic. Living with my dad was difficult; I got tired of being the parent in our relationship. The breaking point was when he did something very upsetting and broke my trust, and I had no choice but to leave.

I ended up living on a friend's couch for a couple of weeks, and then I moved to a shelter. The shelter just offered a bed, meals, and nothing else. Besides the transphobia of most of the staff, they also had policies that did not show they cared for their clients at all. For example, during the days, the shelter would move all of us into one small overcrowded and overheated rec room, and many of us ended up outdoors. I was there during the hottest weeks of summer, and the heat was brutal. It's hard to believe but we were not given water except if we had to take medication, putting many of us at risk of dehydration or heat stroke. I have heard there have been hundreds of complaints filed at that shelter, but their policies are still in place. Suffice to say, I never hope to go back there again.

Fortunately, I was at that first shelter for only a little over a week. A friend connected me with a case manager who worked hard to get me into Daybreak quickly. I lived at the large shelter building for about six months, and I have been living in an off-site apartment for about a month now. I love living entirely on my own and I am working hard to complete my high school diploma and find a temporary job until I settle into a career of art or art therapy.

A place like Daybreak existing in such a small city as Dayton is amazing. The fact that cities ten times bigger than Dayton don't have a homeless shelter solely for youth shows how cool it is for Dayton to have a place like Daybreak. My favorite part of Daybreak has been David's Place, a safe space for LGBTQ+ youth, located inside the building. The director of David's Place has been extremely helpful, open, and honest with me, and has helped me work toward my future, which honestly I didn't think I would have a few years ago.

As wonderful as Dayton is for having a LGBTQ+ safe space for homeless youth, social services in general can do better. They need more trained staff to help the large numbers of clients they serve become independent. Too many people return because the roots of their problems are not addressed before they are discharged.

The problems extend outside of these organizations as well. There's a stigma surrounding homelessness and an attitude that we do not work or do not work hard enough to keep what we have or that we are irresponsible or do not handle our money well. These reasons are true some of the time, but for me and many young people I have met, that is not the case.

We simply cannot accomplish what older people did in the same jobs we have. Minimum wage does not cover rent. Everything I make goes to expenses and I am still not covering all my bills. The system is broken, and something needs to change.

Even though life is not perfect, I am hopeful for the future. I am so incredibly grateful that I have managed to hang on and still be here today. I know the future is never guaranteed, but if I could say anything to my future self, I would like to thank him for being with me 'til the end of the line. I did not believe I would make it to my twenties, let alone imagining a life past that, but I know now that I love myself enough to see a future for myself. I am still learning, growing, and changing, but I know whatever it takes, I am worth it. Just because.

Desperate Times Require Desperate Measures

An anonymous story as told to Angel Bernard

Asking for help can come in many forms, and one way is to *intentionally* become homeless in the shelter system. Being in a unit that one cannot afford is a struggle. Imagine being a single parent with three children, living on a fixed income, and struggling to pay fair market rent. Add the COVID pandemic, a unit in reported disrepair, and the result for this family is to make the final-hour decision to leave their housing for shelter. This desperate measure happened with the hopes that the family will receive an affordable housing voucher.

The growing disparity between housing prices and income is making the goal of finding affordable housing more challenging. This mother of three reached out for COVID-related rent assistance to St. Vincent de Paul (in partnership with the Miami Valley Community Action Agency). Because of the volume of applications, she had waited months for help. Due to the pending court date, her application was prioritized; but by this time the eviction had been granted, and she was scheduled for a moveout by the bailiff the next morning. The team leader spoke to the mother at 9 p.m. the evening prior to the moveout and explained her options. Assuming, of course, that the mother would prefer to stay in her current home, the first option was to reach out to the landlord and seek his willingness to accept the past due balance and three months' forward rent. But because of the late hour, 9 p.m. that evening, the mother insisted that she wanted to leave that night so that the children were not present for the early morning bailiff's arrival. Again, thinking that the mother would prefer to stay in her current home, the team leader continued to explore her available resources to buy some time so that the team could possibly work things out with the landlord. The mother persisted that she had no support in Dayton. She had nowhere they could stay that evening; she denied having a neighbor, a friend, or a family person who would let her stay with them for a few hours in the morning while the team attempted to negotiate with the landlord. She reported her only resource was that someone was in town for only a few hours that evening who would drive her to the shelter.

The team leader then explained a second and third option. If the landlord would not accept the money at that final hour, assuming the mother would provide the necessary paperwork, the second option was that the team could place them temporarily in a hotel while she looked for other housing. The third option was that the family would go to the shelter for assistance on a more long-term basis and be connected with case management.

Assuming, again, that the mother would prefer to keep her family in their current home, the team spent much of their effort on the first option. The mother insisted that the family had to leave the home that night but agreed to allow the team to contact the landlord. The local St. Vincent de Paul conference arranged for the family to stay in a hotel that night. Early the next morning, the team leader communicated with the landlord, who was willing to accept the rent money. However, to the shock of the rent team, the mother declined the rent assistance of all arrearages paid and three months' forward rent. She believed that her only option for a housing voucher was to enter the homeless system.

The next step was transitioning the family to the shelter. Even though the mother had denied any support in Dayton, she could place her older children with their fathers on a temporary basis. A neighbor and friend went back to the apartment to pick up some items left behind. The mother and baby came into the shelter after the hotel assistance ended.

The mother was in the shelter for over nine months, getting her documentation together for assistance with housing and waiting for a voucher. During the time in the shelter, the baby became sick with COVID and RSV, as did the mother. In a communal living space, disease transference is high, especially among children. This put a strain on the mother. She became agitated with the situation, other guests, and shelter staff.

After the seemingly insurmountable barriers she faced, the mother finally obtained a housing voucher in Montgomery County, where she pays a portion of the rent based on her income. The other children will be housed with her as well. She will have ongoing case management during the time she holds her subsidy. The family has been linked with a support system outside of the shelter. With this in place, the family has a stronger chance of sustaining their housing. However, the trauma from eviction and living in the shelter for nine months is a lifelong process that they will need to work through.

Section 3: Discussion Questions

We want to thank the numerous children and people who shared their stories for this section. The causes for eviction and homelessness are many. Many in this section were helped by organizations, friends, strangers, and family. We want to honor these stories and hope understanding the complexity of this problem will enable us to develop more awareness and solutions.

1. *What story (stories) in this section resonated with you? Why?*

2. *As noted in this section, children are experiencing housing insecurity at unprecedented rates in our nation. What surprised you about this collection of voices from children? What can we improve in our community to reduce homelessness, eviction, and housing insecurity trauma for children? What role does*

the McKinney Vento Act play in reducing trauma for children experiencing homelessness?

3. What are the reasons for housing insecurity shared in this section? How do they compare to the stories in the shelter stories section? What stories are missing? What are some of the other reasons people experiencing housing insecurity?

4. What are some of the solutions to housing insecurity suggested in these stories?

5. In looking at the photos included in this section, what role does affordable housing play in reducing housing insecurity in Dayton? In the United States?

Resources to learn and read more about the problem of housing insecurity in the United States (A more detailed resource guide and question guide is provided at the end of this book):

National Low-Income Housing Coalition
https://nlihc.org/

ShelterForce
https://shelterforce.org/

National Center for Homeless Education
https://nche.ed.gov/resources/#:~:text=For%20assistance%20with%20an%20issue,or%20homeless%40serve.org.

SECTION 4

> *"**H**ousing is absolutely essential to human flourishing. Without stable shelter, it all falls apart."*
>
> — *Matthew Desmond*

This section focuses on stories from the social service and housing systems in our community including a landlord perspective, the eviction court perspectives (judge, bailiff, and attorney), and community advocates' perspectives. In this section, we also come to understand the importance of understanding the lived experiences of those who witness the struggles facing those with housing insecurity. We are appreciative of their time in sharing their stories.

Stories From the Housing and Social Services Systems

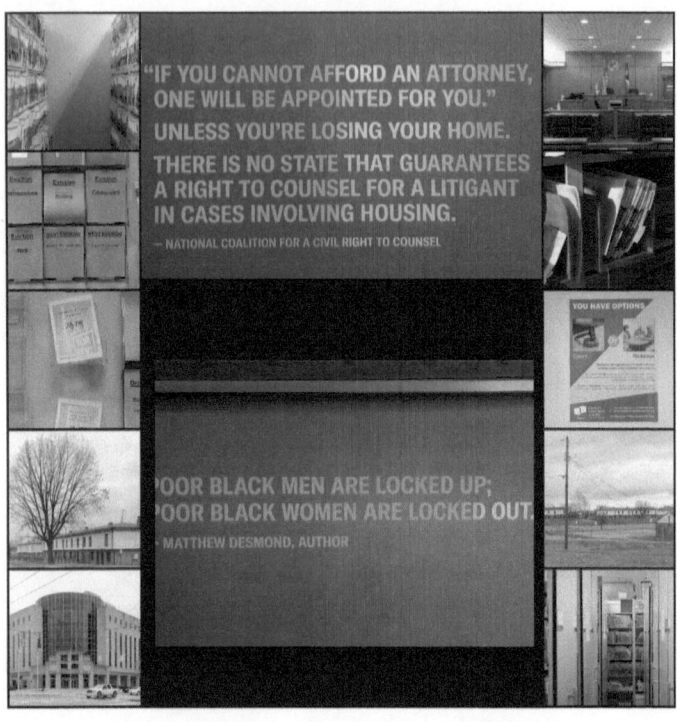

Make Yourself at Home

Landlord/Owner PPG LLC's story as told to Michele Shehee

It's always been my goal to make sure my properties are well-kept and well-maintained before renting them to a family. I'm very proud to say, I've not ever experienced any negative rapport from a tenant I have opened my rentals to. Yes, I have a process of background check, referrals, work history, etc. and I inform the potential tenant this is what I do because if I'm opening my rental home to you, I want you to "make it your own" for you and your family. However, at the same time, I want you to respect what's not yours as well. If you like to paint a wall a different color, no problem, as long as it's painted back to the original color or as close to (with approval) upon the tenant leaving the premises if needed.

My wife and I do what we can to assist those around us to help them become a better version of self, become successful as a good tenant, and who knows, maybe one day, purchase their very own home. However, until we get them there as a homeowner, and we have confirmed the information that has been provided to show that the applicant, their spouse (if married), and any children are safe to rent to, we say "Make yourself at home."

As a Landlord, I have a qualified maintenance crew that I believe is very relevant in order to have your tenants know that I do care about my property, and my crew will confirm the condition of the home if they ever have to visit. Now, I understand the normal wear and tear of occupancy, but there have been times and not many, counting on one hand, there have been where I have made an exception of having more than the said tenant(s) on the lease that may now have a distant relative or parent now living with them. I can recall that I had a house rented out to a family of refugees, and when I was contacted about my property by the organization, I was really excited to help. Of course, there was the period of multiple inspections, contracts with the county/city, lease, etc. that had to be completed before the family of five (father, mother, three children) could move in. This was great because the home was a 3-bedroom,1-bath, large kitchen with galley-table sitting area, a full basement, 2-car garage. This was perfect for the family and a nice "welcome" for them all as they migrated into the area. However, long story short, my wife and I would visit with them to see if there were things they would need, i.e clothing, shoes, etc. At one point they asked for a TV, and we were able to bless them with such. I believe this family really felt welcomed and made it their home much so, their family started to grow.

Landlords, again, we want good tenants that will make us comfortable in knowing our property will be well maintained as we're not there to oversee the property 24/7 but have peace of mind that the property is not going to shambles at least we hope.

As I mentioned before, the family started to grow, not because of the expecting parent(s) pregnancy, but because we realized that the family started inviting other families (refugees) to come and live with them. "Make yourself at home" had become a whole different meaning, I would say. I was getting calls from my maintenance crew that they were getting calls more than the norm of issues at the home. So, one day I decided to visit, and sure enough, the original family of 5 seemed now to be a family of twelve. There were mattresses everywhere, and the basement looked like a mini camping site. I asked who I thought was the original tenant what was going on, and now no one spoke English. Even as today, when I think about this, I must giggle to myself. Now, as a landlord, I couldn't allow this ONLY because I know now the house is in a code violation, especially with the fire department. So, the best thing I had to do, which is not favorable to me, is starting an eviction, because the organization is now telling me they are ok with having the families live together.

Another scenario I've experienced as a landlord was during Covid, all my tenants, unfortunately, suffered a loss of income in some sort of way. However, because of the rapport I have with my tenants, as I share with them during the signing of the lease process, is "Just talk to me and let me know what's going on" we can work something out, but I have no desire to evict you unless that's the last resort and you do not make good on your end. As I heard of the rental assistance being available to the renters, I would share with them about the program.

My wife and I would print them the application and would do our best to work with them, and I'm glad to say, I did not lose a tenant, nor did I have to evict.

Eviction is hard and costly for everyone. The City of Dayton's new rule to make it more difficult to evict is counter-productive because now landlords are going to heighten their standards of who they are going to rent to, causing delays for housing. I know this should further be addressed and I have addressed this concern with the Mayor, because as landlords, we still must pay taxes on our properties, we still maintain our properties, especially if there are codes within the neighborhood and we must pay our mortgages. So, if a tenant is not cooperating with us, as a landlord, then eviction is the last resort. I would rather not unfortunately, it's part of life IF one is not being accountable for their actions and upholding their responsibilities as a tenant. Life is tough, I understand, but when a tenant acts like they are doing you a favor by renting your property, that you have allowed them full access to, to make it their home and disregard the rules of law, then yes, unfortunately, sometimes eviction is necessary.

Horror and Hope: Housing Insecurity Through the Eyes of a Child

Deborah Ferguson's story as told to Heather Johnson-Taylor

There are moments in time that are game-changers.
This story is about one of mine.

It was 1985 and move-in day for our Transitional Housing program. It was warm and sunny, and the staff was grateful for the good weather. It was supposed to rain that day and we were afraid we might have to postpone the move. We hated it when we had delays because all our families were coming from a homeless shelter and were so anxious to finally have their own places.

While the adults unpacked their few belongings, the kids played in the side yard. The excitement of the families was palpable. All the children were squealing with delight as they chased one another. We were excited, too!

As my eyes scanned the yard and parking area, I noticed that the son of our newest family was not with the rest of the kids anymore. He was only ten years old, so I went looking for his mom and dad. I approached his parents and asked the mom, "Where is your son?"

She replied, "He's just unpacking his clothes. He's never had a dresser before."

Oh! What? Did I hear that right?

His mom went on to say he had only ever had boxes because when you get evicted, you have to walk away from your furniture. Sometimes you have to leave everything you own behind. It left me wondering: *What else didn't he have?*

His parents were married and in their 40's. They also had adult children, and when talking about the large age gap between their children, they winked at each other and described the youngest son by saying, "This is Round 2." They had been evicted several times. The wife believed that women should stay home and raise the kids, and the men should work to support the family. This dad did work but he had some serious health issues. He lost his last job for calling in sick too many times. They felt like they were following the rules, but it wasn't enough. Without a reliable source of income, they got behind on their rent and had been evicted several times.

Like many of our families, when people have trouble holding down a job or work under the table, there is no safety net. It's a fact of modern society that we no longer have the extensive social supports that we used to have. Our program was a godsend to these families.

This moment was a turning point for me. Until then, we put so much emphasis on the needs of the parents. Our job was to connect them with the resources they needed to get back on their feet and become self-sufficient. When were we going to talk about this little boy and all the children like him? It caused a great deal of introspection and reflection on my part.

Being passionate about equity and fairness, I wanted to turn my feelings into action. I'm a natural helper. I like to solve problems. I could not be immobilized by my pain. Members of our local and state coalitions began to have honest and open discussions about ways to better serve the children in our shelters and housing programs. As time passed, numerous child advocates in the homeless movement started to collaborate with one another, and our county now has some of the best services for children in the country. As an Assistant Ombudsman for Dayton and Montgomery County, I continue to work as an advocate for fair and just government services.

Looking back, it is difficult to fully understand why that moment had such a profound impact on me. I have this visual of a little boy carrying all of his belongings in a box, and to this very day, every time I talk about this moment, tears flow down my face. I still feel guilty.

I've had to reconcile my feelings with the fact that he appeared to be a nice, happy, and healthy kid. Maybe he was just a little boy who was excited about unpacking his clothes because he never had a dresser before. As someone who works with people navigating the horrors of eviction, it can be difficult to see the joy and the hope sometimes.

We Are Fighting the System

Angel Bernard's story as told to Elizabeth Schmidt

My name is Angel Bernard. I am a licensed social worker. I manage the case management team at two St. Vincent De Paul Shelters in Dayton: The Women and Families Shelter on Apple Street and the Men's Shelter on Gettysburg. I've been with St. Vincent's for five years, and this is where I'm supposed to be, I guess. It's a great organization. We do a lot in the community, not just in the shelters. If somebody's behind on their rent, utility assistance, food pantry, furniture, prayer. You name it, we do it. We're Catholic, so we're allowed to talk about God with the clients ... or Buddha ... whatever religion, or if people don't want to talk about religion, that's okay too.

We take just about everybody. We've got the bigger families coming in. We've got this elderly population coming in. Over the Thanksgiving weekend we took in 18 men. The reasons fluctuate—their family won't accept them; they were released from jail/sober living facilities and evictions. I mean, the list goes on.

We help people find housing and refer them to other agencies to help with other issues. It's a hard job. My team is really good at what they do. They probably don't get paid enough, but they do it because they care. Clients could be our moms, our sisters, our daughters, our sons, or our husbands. They're people. They're human. They have feelings. They have rights.

It's hard to see what people go through on a day-to-day basis. Volunteers will come in and see that people are homeless, but they don't see all the mental health issues and barriers people face as well. Trying to find a job with children. Trying to get daycare, and now they've lost their job because they couldn't get the daycare in time. There's a lot of theft. They've lost their bank cards, and their IDs, and we have to get new ones. They have to have their birth certificate, their ID, and a social security card to be housed through HUD or any subsidized housing for that matter. It's like ten steps back after they've taken five forward. And then you get a group of 200 people, especially men, you've got a lot of testosterone in one room. There's a lot of fighting, a lot of arguing.

We're fighting the system. Subsidized housing through HUD has really long waiting lists. Six months to 5 years. Who wants to stay in a shelter for 5 years while waiting for an apartment? They get frustrated with the process and leave. But if they leave, and they're gone for too long, they've got to start the whole process over when they come back.

That's how things are written in the grants, HUD. And the qualifications to get into housing include criminal background checks. Some men can't get into housing because of one thing that happened twenty years ago. They might be a changed person now. They have changed their life. But no one wants to look at that.

The people who have actually been evicted are so hard to help. I mean we can work with them, but finding a landlord is like pulling teeth. One lady's been here for over a year. We got her a section 8 voucher but trying to get her a landlord has been really really tough. She lived in this apartment for 15 years. Covid happened, and she just couldn't afford it because the rent was raised. The landlord filed for eviction, but it was dismissed in court. So now we're filing all these housing applications, and she's being denied even though the eviction's been dismissed. For this particular lady, we had to write an appeal letter to every landlord. Now her mental health is declining because she's on edge. Depression and anxiety are heightened. Then you've got 200 people going through the same thing in the same shelter.

If they come into the shelter before the eviction is filed, that's great because we can prevent the eviction from happening. We have prevention money. But they're coming to us after the fact—things have been filed in court, and there's no going back.

Evictions are held against people. That's a huge thing. People make mistakes. Evictions pop up on the background checks, even if it was dismissed. Many people have been evicted, and they don't realize it. They say *I was never evicted. I never went to court.* But just because they didn't show up to court doesn't mean a landlord didn't file the eviction. Then you have these people who owe landlords $3000 for court costs and filing fees. So that pops up too. They say *I don't owe money, I left*. But they do owe the money. Then people get denied housing, and they have to stay in a shelter or with family.

So far this year in the homeless system, we're up to 84 deaths. That's the highest number we've ever had. On the first day of winter, we always have a memorial vigil downtown at the courthouse. This year is going to be difficult. There will be 84 pairs of shoes lined up to represent each person. In the shelter, we've had four people pass away this year. One was an overdose—he was 22. Then we had two elderly people, and recently another overdose. They found him on Thanksgiving Day.

It's difficult, but this is my passion. I'm getting my master's in social work. I was selected to go to Washington D.C. to Capitol Hill and talk to Congress about housing. Self-disclosure: I used to be them. I have a history of addiction. I have a history of homelessness and the prison system. When I finally got sober and moved to Dayton, I asked God *What am I supposed to do?* And He said *Stay in Dayton*. I knew I had to be here. The opportunity to help someone that I used to be ... I can't even explain it. The moment when someone signs a lease, and they're so thankful. That's what it's about.

Not Everyone Believes in Second Chances

Danielle's story as told to Heidi Arnold

I n 2015, I had no steady income. I longed to be independent. I was a young, single mom. I had just told my boyfriend of four years to get lost. I had not completed high school. I was dancing at a club. But the good news was that I had been introduced to a landlord who consented to rent an apartment to me.

I was so happy the day I moved in all my stuff by myself. My daughter, then four years old, and I would have a place to live. I didn't care that the landlord was entranced by the fact that I danced for money at a club. I had seen his kind before. I was nervous though. So many questions ran through my mind: How could I survive without my boyfriend? How could I pay the rent and utilities and buy food with such an unreliable way to earn money? I thought I needed my boyfriend to make it, so I asked him back into my life. He came back but with drugs and alcohol and friends who liked to party.

Within days, my neighbor, an older white man, began to complain about the noise, the music inside my apartment as well as the comings and goings of my boyfriend and his friends. Over the course of the year we lived there, the neighbor man called the police 58 times. He filmed our doorway and yelled at us with a microphone to ensure that we heard him. He took pictures of us and called Child's Services.

I reported his behavior to the landlord, and the Riverside police did nothing to us because we were doing nothing wrong. I noticed he only called the police when my boyfriend was around. I finally put two and two together to realize the neighbor did not like that my boyfriend was Black. Because the neighbor made himself a pest to the police, the officers threatened to label the apartment building a nuisance if they had to come one more time.

Unfortunately, for me, the landlord was exhausted by the visits and would not get rid of the real problem, and he decided I had to move out. I received the notice and was out *before* the eviction date. Later, I found out that the eviction was filed in the courts—even though it shouldn't have been—and was now a part of my record.

I moved to another apartment, not far from there, and life spun out of control. Due to my presence in the apartment and activities unbeknownst to me, my boyfriend's behavior caused me to be convicted of a crime for which I served five years in prison.

During my time, I earned my GED, took college classes, and participated in an intensive six-month drug and alcohol program. Upon my release in 2021, I lived with my mother and my 10-year-old daughter,

Mia. Within two weeks, I secured a good job. My next step was to find housing, but I knew it would be a problem with a felony on my record as well as that eviction label.

Because of my connections with the drug and alcohol program, I was referred to Miami Valley Housing Opportunities (MVHO) and found out the eviction had mysteriously been removed! With the help of MVHO, a nonprofit organization focused on finding permanent housing for the most vulnerable, I was living in my own apartment four months later. They helped with the registration and background check and served as a middleman for me.

MVHO paid the deposit for my apartment and the first four months of rent. They gave me pots and pans and a microwave, kitchen supplies, rugs for the bathroom and a shower curtain. They even gave me a bed for my daughter and a kitchen table. I am so thankful for their help.

At the time, I was working but had not yet saved any money. Today, I pay 75% of the rent and MVHO pays the rest. I now work two jobs, and my daughter stays with me part of the week on my days off. I had no independence before, but now I have everything I need.

Recently, I began to search for a place that's a bit bigger and closer to my work. I did the legwork of finding a landlord who had compassion and understood my predicament of having the label of felon on my record. We sat down and had a conversation, so I could tell him exactly what happened and why I spent five years in prison. I told my story, and the landlord was willing to give me a chance.

MVHO graduated me to another level in their program and will again be helping me with rent until I am able to take it on myself. I am excited to be productive again and making strides. Staring at my daughter through glass for 18 months, and then not being able to see or touch her at all because of COVID restrictions, I lived almost three years of my life without physically touching my child. We have so much time to make up for.

Not everyone is going to be willing to see your change or progress. Not everyone believes in second chances. I was turned down at least five times before finding my next home. I want my daughter to see me never giving up when the going gets tough.

The Bailiff Who Conducts Evictions--Be Respectful to All

An anonymous story as told to Stanley Hirtle

I have had a 44-year career in law enforcement; the last four years, I was a court bailiff charged with enforcing evictions. People think of bailiffs as being in the courtroom, but there are also "outside bailiffs" who serve legal documents and conduct evictions.

I see both sides of the eviction problem, as I was once a landlord and later managed property for my father when he was no longer able to do so. Every eviction situation is different, and you never know what you are going to find. Ninety-nine percent of the time the people are cooperative. It's important to treat everyone with respect, even though they have got themselves in a spot where they are being evicted. Some property owners are bailiff happy, puff out their chests and verbally abuse the tenants they are evicting. We tell them to go sit down. Sometimes there are disagreements between the property owner and tenant over what has happened. Those need to be raised beforehand in court before the judge, not in front of us.

This is how it works. First, the property owner goes to court and proves to the judge he is entitled to evict a tenant. The most common cause is non-payment of rent, but there can be others, too. Then the property owner files a request for eviction. The bailiffs get the writ of eviction, and we post a notice on the property saying what day we are coming to evict. By law we have seven to 10 days to perform the eviction. Most commonly we attach the notice to the property, but sometimes we hand it to the tenant.

Occasionally, there is an emergency court hearing as late as the afternoon before the eviction. The court administrators let us know if an eviction is canceled after the emergency hearing.

We schedule eviction times based on where the evictions are located, to minimize our driving around. The property owner has to call us by 8:30 the morning we are scheduled to come out to confirm our arrival time. If they don't call by 8:30, we get on the road and they have to file a new request. Forty to fifty percent of the time, the property owner doesn't call us and we don't go to evict, because we do not know if the tenant has moved out, if they have settled with the property owner to stay, or if the property owner just failed to call us in time.

The property owner needs to be there at the actual eviction. Sometimes, they have a locksmith to take out the lock and let us in. We do not break down doors or force entry. Years ago we used to bring movers to set out the tenant's belongings, but we no longer do that. We give the tenant 15 minutes to get their belongings out. I tell them to get their cell phone, wallet, medicine and what they really need. By law once the set out has occurred, any property the tenant leaves behind becomes the property of the landlord. This is in the notice of eviction that we leave at the property so the tenant knows in advance. In practice, many times the property owner agrees to let the tenant come back and get some property. However, if the tenant does not keep their appointment, that is usually the last chance.

Once the property owner gets the door open, we announce we are court bailiffs. We make the tenants stand outside or, in bad weather, just inside the front door. Then we go through the house looking for people. There might be other tenants or squatters. There might be contraband. There might be animals.

Some of my memorable evictions are:

- I entered a house, announced my presence and went through the rooms. In the last room a lady was in bed asleep. I saw her and closed the door. She said I was a day early and she had until tomorrow to move. It turned out she was correct and I had made a mistake. We left and returned the next day. The house was totally vacant and she had cleaned it so well you could have rented it right then and there.

- I remember a lady being evicted who was clearly mentally challenged. She had a payee who received her money and paid her rent for her. I called the payee. They had supposedly sent a crew to look and see if she was still living there. The crew had reported that she was not living there, so the payee had not paid the rent and the lady was now being evicted. It was obvious to me that the lady had been living there for some time, so I don't know whether the crew had made a mistake or not. Anyway, there was nothing I could do about it at that point as the property owner went through with the eviction.

- The lady being evicted told me a church had agreed to catch up her rent. She was watching television and was clearly not expecting to move. The tenant called the church and had trouble getting through to the pastor. When she did talk to him he sounded evasive, but denied having agreed to pay her rent. Again, all I could do was go through with the eviction. The property owner did give her an additional week to move her belongings out.

- The tenant was supposed to fix the property in lieu of paying rent. He was eventually evicted. He used the property to repair cars, and when I arrived he was working on one with the motor half assembled. His brother came by and said, "Man, I told you you needed to be out." I gave him until the property owner changed all the locks, which took about an hour. He put his clothes, computer, and tools into three cars that were outside the property. He didn't do anything with the motor he was working on and the car it came from, which belonged to someone else, and I don't know what happened to that property.

- I had to evict a mother with three kids. They hadn't moved or packed anything. The youngest child was about eight years old. She started giving the others orders of where they should put what belongings. It was like she, instead of me, was the one running the show. I remember her standing there with her stuffed animal and her backpack, getting the job done.

- Lastly, in my most memorable eviction, I knew things would be difficult when I saw cockroaches on the post outside the house. When I entered the kitchen there were cockroaches on the walls, the counters, and everywhere. When I went into the dining room, a cascade of cockroaches fell from the ceiling. I refused to go any further into the house and told the owner she would need to get exterminators with hazmat suits to get rid of them. There was also a mother pit bull that had 10 puppies in the garage. We backed out slowly and called Animal Control to come get them. I did see the house was back on the rental market six months later.

I see the need for evictions. Eviction tells tenants, not just the one being evicted but the others as well, what can happen if you don't pay your rent or are a bad tenant. Sometimes the neighbors are glad when they see a bad tenant evicted.

There can be serial evictees, whose name you see several times on the docket. Some tenants pay their first rent and deposit, then stop paying and have to be evicted. They know they didn't intend to pay any more rent. There was another lady who wouldn't pay her rent until we showed up to evict her, and then she paid. The third time she did this the property owner refused to take her money, as is his right, and she was evicted.

There are also serial evictors. Some property owners induce tenants to move into places that are pig sties and promise to repair them, but then don't. Often the tenants stop paying rent and the property owner evicts them. There is a court process where a tenant can pay rent into court escrow until the property owner repairs the property, but more often the tenant just doesn't pay and gets evicted. In escrow court the judge can order repairs, or sometimes the judge rules for the property owner and gives them the rent money. We don't deal with the escrow process as outside bailiffs, so I don't know how well it works in practice.

A few property owners have been known to make arrangements with tenants in exchange for sexual favors and then don't follow through. We are stuck in the middle as we are enforcing what the courts decide. One time a guy yelled at me from the next house that I was an Uncle Tom working for the man and I shouldn't put brothers out in the street. I told him, "if you don't want to see me, then pay your rent."

During the COVID pandemic there was a building full of tenants and no one was paying their rent. They were all medical workers, nurses, and the like. They said there was an eviction moratorium because of COVID, which was true, but what was going to happen when the moratorium was over and the rent was due? There is some COVID rent relief for tenants but most people don't know about it or how to apply for it. When we get there to evict them it is too late to apply.

On the other hand, we canceled an eviction after a tenant got COVID relief from an agency to pay all the back rent plus six months in advance.

In the end, as a bailiff you do your job, what you are paid to do. You can't make everything right, but you are dealing with people and you need to treat them with respect.

From the Eyes of A Magistrate

An anonymous story as told to Christine Trotter

I've been a magistrate for the Dayton Municipal Court system for seventeen years, hearing criminal, traffic, eviction, and small claims civil cases. My job is to hear both sides and determine who is being truthful and who to rule in favor of, according to the laws. I can't rule based on my opinion. However, that doesn't mean I'm not human, that I don't see the pain and anguish of those who come into my courtroom.

I learned long ago not to take my work home with me and to keep my face free of emotion when hearing a case. Sometimes though, eviction cases can be tough to hear. Some tenants simply can't pay their rent, or they get so far behind and can't catch up. You never really know what someone is going through, how they are surviving or trying to, and you're the one who has to tell them the law says they must move. It's not just a tenant's livelihood at stake, but a landlord's too.

Therefore, I can't stress enough how important it is for any party in an eviction court case to know their rights, the laws, and how they apply to them.

This housing crisis we're in—we've been in it a long, long time. Prior to the COVID pandemic, people experienced rent and mortgage rate hikes, job loss, living paycheck to paycheck, life-altering situations happening, landlords doing illegal things, tenants taking advantage, and so on. Add to that our current situation of trying to recover from the pandemic: Rent is higher than most mortgages out there. The housing inventory is low, which stems from the 2019 tornadoes that ravaged Dayton and other surrounding areas. We have been faced with more job loss and a weakened economy that many people never experienced before in their lives. All these factors add weight to a crisis that already existed – and now it just remains stagnant.

Most cases I hear are simple: a tenant has not paid their rent, and they know it, and no matter what reason there might be, or how nice a tenant is, a landlord can't sustain their own livelihood by allowing a tenant to live rent-free. Most landlords go about handling evictions legally—they give a notice, they contact the court, they show up in court, and either they mediate with the tenant and work something out, or the tenant must vacate. It's never easy telling someone they have to leave their home. With each eviction, we are adding to an already exorbitant number that exists because of other issues plaguing our communities. This might make the eviction process itself feel and seem inhumane, but something that many don't realize is that laws are in place to protect everyone.

An extreme situation occurred in my courtroom that reminds me of the importance of such laws, and my role in upholding them by holding those accountable who should be. It's not always the tenant at fault for something. There are landlords out there who might take shortcuts, and they will use any means necessary to falsely protect themselves—like this very situation:

For a tenant to file an escrow, their rent must be current, and it must be filed before an eviction is filed against them. Escrows usually involve a landlord who hasn't fixed something they are responsible for. The law requires that the tenant serve the landlord a 30-day notice in writing indicating that the tenant will be placing rent in escrow if they do not fix what is broken. If the repair involves an emergency, no written notice is required prior to filing the escrow, and the parties appear in court as soon as possible. "Emergency" examples are not having water or heat. In this case, a tenant filed an emergency escrow for not having hot water, and they had also tried to pay their rent, but the landlord refused it.

The landlord claimed there was hot water when the tenant insisted there wasn't. My bailiff went out to the property to find there was hot water—but only because the landlord snuck in and turned it up, and then after my bailiff left, the landlord turned the hot water back down, and he removed the front door to the tenant's apartment—which we learned about all of this from another emergency filed by the tenant. I contacted the landlord and told him he needed to return to court for another emergency hearing. He admitted he took the door off. I told him he needed to put it back on or the tenant would be staying in a hotel that he'd foot the bill for.

He put the door back on, but the bottom hinge was broken, so the door still wasn't shutting all the way, and it still put the tenant and their belongings in a precarious situation. You can't expect a tenant to feel safe being exposed like that. In between all this, the hot water was still being turned up and down, and the tenant kept contacting the court asking us what they should do. I decided to go out there myself with my bailiff, and sure enough, the hot water was up. During that visit, we also discovered that the apartment building was ripe with roaches - everywhere.

It turned out that the tenant was in the process of moving, but they were current on their rent and still living in their apartment. They were elderly, on their own, and even though they were moving, that apartment was still their home, and they were not being provided with the necessities the landlord was obligated to, by law, provide. The landlord's logic was that since the tenant was moving, they didn't need hot water—or a front door, apparently.

I ruled in favor of the tenant, telling the landlord that he would not receive his rent. Of course, this upset the landlord to no end. He then turned around and gave the tenant a three-day eviction notice on the grounds of "harboring an extra person" in their apartment, he filed an objection to my ruling on not receiving his rent, and then he filed an eviction on the tenant for non-payment of rent. I explained to him that from the very beginning, his antics and shenanigans were nothing short of absolute and utter harassment toward his tenant.

This was the most extreme case and the worst case of harassment toward a tenant that I have seen in my time on the bench, and from a landlord who is a regular in the courtroom at that. However extreme a situation it was though, it does demonstrate how the laws are in place to protect everyone—tenant and/or landlord.

Should this have even happened in the first place? Is there a way we can prevent such situations? Is there a way we see fewer evictions in our courtrooms? How can we ease the housing crisis instead of constantly adding to it? There's no one answer or even an easy answer to any of these questions, but I can offer some advice.

Whether you're a landlord or a tenant facing an eviction situation, seek help. We have a Legal Aid in Montgomery County. Get your own lawyer, and if you can't afford one, try to get a consultation. There's also a self-help center in the courthouse with brochures full of information on an assortment of topics. The court also offers mediation, so sometimes, cases don't even make it to the courtroom.

Educate yourselves on the laws and your rights. Use Google to find information. Be aware of the escrow process and how it works. If more tenants know how escrow works, they might avoid eviction by legally forcing landlords to fix what they need to. If you create any documentation, make sure you word things correctly. Cases can easily be dismissed, or you could easily end up owing lots of money to someone because an important document, like an eviction notice, was worded incorrectly. Educate high school and college students on housing options, budgeting, finances, and the laws regarding renting, leases, escrows, and such.

I wish there was a better balance between powers. I wish there were fewer flaws in systems we rely on to live. Yet, we remain human, facing processes that we don't understand, processes that we don't always ask to be a part of. Our community members can best serve their needs and the needs of others by practicing self-perseverance and integrity. This includes both landlords and tenants. This is what will keep us human.

Section 4: Discussion Questions

*W*e want to thank the many people who offered to share stories for this section. We are especially grateful to the landlord, the bailiff, the magistrate, and the lawyer who wanted to share their perspectives and experiences. The eviction court system and issues facing tenants remain a serious concern for housing justice advocates. In this section, you will have an opportunity to see various perspectives on eviction and the court system. Finally, we also appreciate those who work daily as social workers and community advocates to try to provide a safety net for the system that many think is broken. These advocates make a difference in the lives of so many.

1. What role do landlords play in the housing insecurity crisis in America? In our community? What makes for a "good" landlord? What makes for a good "tenant"? What are some

of the issues in our community with absent landlords? Many note that the legal system favors the landlord. Why is this the case? What might need to be changed to make the legal system fairer to tenants?

2. In reviewing the stories by the bailiff, the magistrate, and the lawyer, what did you learn about eviction court? Did you know that tenants in our community have no right to counsel? Why do you think people in poverty are not given the right to counsel in civil court in the United States? Is this fair? Is this just? What other types of civil court cases might a person in poverty be at a disadvantage without a right to counsel? What questions do you have about eviction court and processes?

3. Did you know there is racial disparity in eviction filings in the United States and Dayton, Ohio? Why do you think families of color are more likely to experience eviction? What role does racism play in the housing injustice system? What can we do as a community?

4. What role do community advocates and social workers play in helping those struggling with housing insecurity? What types of emotional labor do they work with day in and day out? How might we better support them in their work in our communities?

Resources to learn and read more about the problem of eviction in the United States (A more detailed resource guide and question guide is provided at the end of this book):

National Coalition for Civil Right to Counsel: www.civilrighttocounsel.org

The Eviction Research Network: https://evictionresearch.net/

The Eviction Lab: https://evictionlab.org/

SECTION 5

> "A lot of people do not look at housing as a human right, but it is."

— Jimmy Carter

Stories About Housing as a Human Right

Lot by Lot, House by House, Block by Block

Dee Wooding's story as told to Hannah Priebe

"Oh, maybe they're going to do something about this neighborhood."

As a little girl growing up on Hoover Avenue, that's what I thought every time somebody'd knock on the door with a piece of paper and a little clipboard, asking you questions as if they're going to do something.

But they knocked on our door with that little pencil and paper and clipboard over and over and over for years, and nothing happened.

In 2019, I heard from an older lady I grew up with, Jeannette, one of the first African Americans who moved into Westwood. She was out there, very concerned about the decline of the neighborhood. She doesn't drive anymore because she's considered legally blind, so she was catching this bus stop, but the bus stop had all these overgrown shrubs and trees, and it was just a blighted bus stop. You couldn't even enjoy sitting at the bus stop because of all the overgrown shrubs and trees. So, she started to clean it herself. She'd walk two blocks just to clean that bus stop up with her own lawn mower and hedge trimmers.

She told me how she had reached out to people, but nobody was caring. They were just letting her do this alone. She was telling me that, and I was like "No, not on my watch." So, we drove to the bus stop, and I said there's just no way this could be.

That's how the Westwood Right Project CDC got started. We had our first cleanup right around that bus stop. And that bus stop has never been cleaner or looked better than it does today.

There are all of these people in Westwood possibly facing eviction because they are paying this extremely high rent for these very small one- or two-bedroom homes because investors have infiltrated these poor, impoverished neighborhoods and bought up all these homes. And now the residents there don't have the opportunity to own, so they're forced to rent. With our project, we buy blighted homes and renovate them to be almost like a brand new home. Then, we'll make it available for a homeownership opportunity at half of what they would pay in rent, so they're not facing those low-quality housing issues and possible eviction at the whim of the landlord.

It's hard work, but if we don't do it, then who will? These Black and brown communities are being grossly neglected and disinvested. When it comes to the funding, the resources and the investments...there is no equity. Period. If there were, a lot of these issues would be solved. If there weren't predatory lending, redlining, and other housing injustice issues, of course 800 homes wouldn't be boarded up. You wouldn't have all the people paying rent and facing eviction.

When we go for the funding, we can't get the funding. It's like all these other major nonprofits get the funding for these communities, while African American-led organizations are not receiving funding to do the work in our communities. Why isn't the funding coming through?

They'll say "Well, you're new," so it's almost like we're being punished for being new. Are you kidding me? We're new because no one else is trying to address the decline of the neighborhood. If we sat back and said "Oh, we might as well not even try" because they said they're not going to fund us, then this much wouldn't have been done.

While the neighborhood is not receiving funding and other resources to stabilize and revitalize, the outside investors are coming in like vultures buying up the homes and becoming slum landlords while charging these extremely high rents. Most of these people, they've not been given a chance to own a home, something that other people just take for granted, like it's almost their birthright to own a home. My motivation is to know that eventually there's going to be someone who now can never have to worry about facing homelessness or being evicted because they will be the proud owner of a home.

I do it for Dorothy, whose only view from her living room was a dilapidated home right across the street, who has since passed away. For Shirley, 82 years old, out there in the heat mowing the vacant lot next to her. For Linda, facing eviction after just losing her husband. For Jeannette, who would still be at any cleanup even though her health has declined even more.

So, until we get all of Hoover and Westwood stabilized and revitalized, we'll keep fighting the blight lot by lot, house by house, and block by block.

A Righteous Fight to Eradicate Housing Insecurity

Commissioner Shenise Turner-Sloss's story as told to Tennille Love-Frost

My mother's relationship with my stepfather was often filled with uncertainties. For a long time when my mother and stepfather were together, our family struggled with housing. We often had to move from place to place because of my stepfather's inability to provide housing. My family was a part of the working poor, and I did not experience secure housing until my mother divorced my stepfather. However, I was not alone; these unfortunate circumstances were not uncommon, especially in areas with a high poverty rate. Several of my friends also struggled with housing insecurities as a result of their parents' experiences with low-wage jobs, unemployment, substance abuse and domestic violence.

My paternal grandmother recognized my family's immediate need for housing, and she had a dear friend whose elderly uncle's house would be available due to him transitioning to a nursing facility. My grandmother helped broker a deal for my mother to land purchase/lease contract a house in Residence Park from her friend for a nominal purchase price. Ten years old was the first time in my childhood that my family would have a decent, stable home, and I attribute that to my grandmother, my grandmother's friend, Ms. Clarissa, and my mother.

Perhaps it was the innocence of me being a child that I was not fully aware of experiencing and surviving housing insecurity until I became a young adult working in housing and community development with the City of Dayton. It was at that moment I recognized that housing insecurity was a reality for many. As I traveled throughout the city, in many neighborhoods because of the work that I did at that time, it was brought to my attention by a co-worker that I had lived in many areas considered unstable. As a child I viewed it as a badge of experience of being well-versed in Dayton neighborhoods; however, as an adult, it was a sign of housing insecurity.

As a new college graduate returning from Nashville, TN, a city that was experiencing major economic development, I was blown away by the devastation that I saw around Dayton. Within four to five years, formerly self-sufficient communities were now desolate—no grocery stores, empty shopping plazas, and a myriad of boarded up vacant houses.

It is disheartening to know that people are forced to live in conditions where structures are boarded up with tarps on roofs. Many neighborhoods literally had one extension cord running from one house to another, children's toys and bikes strewn in the yard with buckets outside. These were all clear indicators that these structures were occupied with families. These sights were gut punching because of the realization that "this" had become a new norm in many Dayton neighborhoods. As a human being, you have to ask yourself, "What are we doing, and what are we not doing for people to live in these conditions?"

This is why I am so committed to working to make housing a human right. This is what Dr. Martin Luther King Jr. was advocating for in 1964 and '65 during the Poor People's Campaign—we must treat people with dignity! People must have access to education, employment, as well as decent and affordable housing. We have predatory and insufficient affordable housing that leads us to ponder if this is somewhere that you and I would prefer to live? This is why I am so appreciative of the work that the University of Dayton, Human Rights Center is championing along with many community leaders and residents.

Serving as a Dayton City Commissioner, I attribute my passion and commitment to the continuous work towards increasing the well-being of all residents as my motivation to "do and be the work."

The Commission's Housing Informal Resolution is a framework that speaks to the Commission's commitments and need to treat housing as a human right; however, this is not enough—we need enforceable policy. How do we make sure that resolutions are enforced—by putting in the dollars, resources, and manpower, this is how we can make the impact in our communities. We can not wait for the federal government to come and save us. We must start and build it from the ground up as a grassroots effort. *We* must put money behind the policies.

In *their* (residents') experiences, I see *my* personal experiences. I know these are challenges not specific to Dayton, OH, but across the country, and we have to figure it out—we can not wait. We can not expect people to be productive without a roof over their head. We can not expect a child to go to school and perform, take a test, and sit at a desk when they're "couch surfing" or do not know if they can return to auntie's house or back to the shelter. Dayton Public Schools (DPS) has a very high number of students that are homeless. Dayton has one of the highest poverty rates in the nation, and we should be doing whatever is necessary to decrease that poverty rate. The data shows that we are still dealing with the effects of redlining. We can not continue to use flowery language to get federal funds and do nothing to address the issues that cause poverty in our community. Poverty is a root cause for the mental health crisis—all these issues are related. These are real issues that adults and children are dealing with, and it's not as simple as, "They just need to get an education, or go to work"—people are trying to figure it out the best way they know how. People are asking, "Where do I lay my head, and how do I make sure my kids have a safe place to lay their heads?"

I am seeing that the conversation around housing is being pushed to the forefront; however, we have to do more because it's getting worse. Even now, I am working with a resident of Northwest Dayton that is being taken advantage of by a management company. She came to my office with a trifold full of complaint letters filed with the City of Dayton, documentation and pictures of her living conditions, such as the basement being flooded and backfilled with feces—it was horrible! Yet, she is paying over $1,300 in rent. So, we must be intentional with our approach to educate our residents of places they can go for help, and we must also hold these owners and management companies accountable for the condition of their properties. However, let me be clear and impartial: we have irresponsible people on both sides, so we have to put safeguards in place to hold everyone accountable in all aspects.

My goal is to propose legislation that utilizes local, state, and federal funding to implement best practices that address the housing crisis. In cities such as Toledo, Pittsburgh, and Detroit, innovative and responsive legislation is influencing the creation of programming for the right to counsel, housing trust funds, and policy-based budgets are being used to address this issue. Homelessness and poor living conditions are unacceptable—and there is plenty of work for ALL of us to do to ensure that everyone has a decent home and opportunity.

Final Discussion

This collection of lived experiences and stories was, in part, created in hopes of supporting more awareness and dialogue in our community to affect social change. ***There are guided discussion questions at the end of each section, and we hope groups will first start with those questions as part of a dialogue group.*** The questions provided below are meant to be discussed as a broader discussion of housing justice and social change. *These are some suggested questions, and we hope that you will also create your own questions and ways of discussing these stories. You may also want to allow for time in your groups for members to share their own housing insecurity stories. Many people in the United States have experienced a housing crisis at some point in their lives, and community storytelling may be a way to build trust and empathy in your own circles.*

1. What does the concept of "home" mean to you? What did it mean to some of the people who shared stories in this collection? What role does a sense of "place" play in individual and community well-being? Think about having members of your group draw their concept of home and share it with

the group as an ice-breaker to start this discussion, or perhaps bring an image or photo to share.

2. What did you learn more about from reading this collection of stories? Did you learn new information? Did your perspectives on this issue change in any way? What do you want to know more about after reading these stories?

3. What stories spoke most to you and why? Where did you feel the most connected to the storyteller, and when did you feel the least connected? What role do you think "empathy" plays in affecting social change in the lives of those experiencing housing insecurity in America?

4. Why do children experience such high rates of eviction and homelessness in the United States? How can we mitigate the trauma children experience from poverty and systemic racism? What is your community doing to support children struggling with housing insecurity? What services is your local school providing?

5. This book includes a collection of photographs that, in many ways, symbolize many of the issues in this book. We intentionally chose NOT to photograph people in crisis situations. We appreciate that people made a choice to share their stories but wanted to honor their stories as much as possible. In looking back through the photos included in this book, what are some of the photos that "spoke" to you or you found problematic? What symbols and messages do the abandoned homes tell us about affordable hous-

ing? What messages do all the eviction files in a court office tell us about eviction? If you could take a photo to symbolize your thoughts on housing justice, what would it be?

6. Unfortunately, there is often *shame* associated with being poor in America. Also, as you learned from many of the stories, people in poverty are often treated as criminals in our eviction housing systems and our shelters. Many noted this shame in their stories and noted the trauma they experienced from the places and people that are supposed to be lending assistance. How can we reduce the trauma and discrimination that those in poverty often face in our communities? What can we do as a community to humanize those who are often dehumanized by our systems and policies?

7. Unfortunately, both poverty and racism play a role in the stories of housing insecurity. Why are people from marginalized communities disproportionately affected by housing insecurity? What can we do to stop this from happening in our neighborhoods and communities? What role does racial justice play in the story of housing justice? What other communities are disproportionately affected by homelessness and eviction? What types of change are needed?

8. What are the major housing insecurity issues discussed in this book? List them all. Once you have listed them, take time to discuss the causes and issues that are not included in this book.

9. There are many causes of homelessness noted in these stories; however, most agree that the most pressing problem is the lack of decent, affordable housing in the United States. What would it take to have more affordable housing in your community? What would this look like? How can we make sure everyone has access to affordable housing?

10. Should housing be a human right? If so, what would this look like in the United States? What is your vision of housing as a human right?

11. After your group discusses this book, before you close your dialogue session, please take time to create a "Blueprint to Reduce Eviction and Housing Insecurity in your Community." Identify 10 things your community could do to affect change.

12. Once you develop a community list, think about making your own personal list. What can you do to help your community and those most affected by housing insecurity? What are some ways you can volunteer or become active in human rights and housing justice work?

Resources on hosting a community book read:
Scholastic Educators—Discussion Guides
https://www.scholastic.com/content/dam/scholastic/educators/discussion-guides/community-reads-program-guide.pdf

Resources on Lived Experience and Social Change:

The Lived Experience Organization
https://thelivedexperience.org/

The Sheila McKenchie Foundation
https://smk.org.uk/power-lived-experience-and-social-change-the-story-so-far/
https://www.socialchangeinnovators.com/file/?f=384

Activating Lived Experience to Create Social Change
https://www.ted.com/talks/sunny_dhadley_activating_lived_experience_to_create_social_change

Ganesh, Shiv & Zoller, Heather. (2012). Dialogue, activism, and democratic social change. *Communication Theory*. 22. 10.1111/j.1468-2885.2011.01396.x.

Clancy, Sharon; Harman, Kerry; & Jones, Iain (2022). Special issue on lived experience, learning, community activism and social change. *Studies in the Education of Adults*, 54:2, 123-127, DOI: 10.1080/02660830.2022.2105551

Resource Guide

Sinclair Community College's Library created a library guide for eviction and housing insecurity:
https://libguides.sinclair.edu/eviction

Princeton University has created a good resource on housing in America:
https://princetonlibrary.org/housing-in-america-a-resource-guide/

Websites with suggested books, films, and podcasts to learn more:
Books, Films, and Podcasts - Eviction and Housing Instability - LibGuides at Sinclair Community College
https://www.humanrightscareers.com/issues/books-about-homelessness/
https://lafh.org/lafhblog/reading-list
Gimme Shelter - CalMatters

https://www.nytimes.com/2021/09/30/books/review/invisible-child-dasani-andrea-elliott.html

Simulations/games:

https://risehomestories.com/dots-home/resources/

https://playspent.org/html/

Additional Resources

Need Help? Montgomery County

Homelessness Prevention—

Rental Assistance Resources

https://miamivalleycap.org/application-portal/

Mortgage Assistance Resources

Homeownership Center Mortgage Assistance Program

Homeless? Need Shelter?

Montgomery County Shelter & Outreach Providers

Daybreak

605 S. Patterson Blvd.

Dayton, OH 45402

24-hour emergency shelter for youth ages 10-21.

Crisis Hotline: (937) 461-1000

Administrative Offices: (937) 395-4600

Gettysburg Gateway for Men

1921 S. Gettysburg Ave.

Dayton, OH 45417

24-hour emergency shelter for single men.

Contact: (937) 222-7350

PATH Street Outreach

Outreach to single adults and families who are living on the street or unsheltered places.

Contact: (937) 263-4449 ext. 410

St. Vincent Gateway for Women & Families
120 W. Apple Street
Dayton, OH 45402
24-hour emergency shelter for single women and families, including families with children and families without children.
Contact: (937) 461-7837

YWCA Dayton Domestic Violence Shelter
24-hour shelter for victims of domestic violence, sexual assault, stalking, and human trafficking.
Crisis Hotline: (937) 222-SAFE (7233)
Email: dvcrisis@ywcadayton.org

Street Card

The Street Card Resource Guide is designed to provide homeless persons with information on needed services for which they may be eligible. The Street Card Resource Guide contains a limited listing of services in Montgomery County.

Street Card - Color

Street Card - B&W

Street Card Folding Instructions

We welcome you to download, print, and distribute the Street Card.

To receive additional information on resources, please contact HelpLink at 2-1-1.

https://www.mcohio.org/departments/human_services_planning_and_development/homeless_solutions/homeless_assistance_resources.php#:~:text=Contact%3A%20(937)%20222%2D7350&text=Outreach%20to%20single%20adults%20and,the%20street%20or%20unsheltered%20places.

Need Help with Eviction? Tenant Rights? Housing Discrimination?

https://dayton-unitedway.org/get-help-now/

Advocates for Basic Legal Equality

https://www.ablelaw.org/

Dayton Mediation Center: Landlord/Tenant Mediation

https://www.daytonmediationcenter.org/landlord-tenant-mediation

Miami Valley Fair Housing

https://www.mvfairhousing.com/

Student at Sinclair Community College?(Also good resource guide for anyone in Montgomery/Warren County)

https://www.sinclair.edu/student-life/wellness/resources/

About The Facing Project

The Facing Project is a 501(c)(3) nonprofit that creates a more understanding and empathetic world through stories that inspire action. The organization provides tools and a platform for everyday individuals to share their stories, connect across differences, and begin conversations using their own narratives as a guide. The Facing Project has engaged more than 7,500 volunteer storytellers, writers, and actors who have told more than 1,500 stories that have been used in grassroots movements, in schools, and in government to inform and inspire action.

In addition, stories from The Facing Project are published in books through The Facing Project Press and are regularly performed on The Facing Project Radio Show on NPR.

Learn more at facingproject.com.
Follow us on Twitter and Instagram @FacingProject,
and on Facebook at TheFacingProject.

www.ingramcontent.com/pod-product-compliance
Lightning Source LLC
LaVergne TN
LVHW041842070526
838199LV00045BA/1405